D0061910

THE FIRST AMERICAN FURNITURE FINISHER'S MANUAL

A Reprint of
"The Cabinet-Maker's Guide" of 1827

edited by
ROBERT D. MUSSEY, JR.

DOVER PUBLICATIONS, INC., NEW YORK

Published in Canada by General Publishing
Company, Ltd., 30 Lesmill Road, Don Mills, Toronto,
Ontario.
Published in the United Kingdom by Constable
and Company, Ltd.

This Dover edition, first published in 1987, is an
unabridged, unaltered republication of the work as
published by Jacob B. Moore, Concord, N.H., in
1827, under the title *The Cabinet-Maker's Guide: or
Rules and Instructions in the Art of Varnishing* . . . .
A new Introduction and Glossary of Terms have
been written specially for the Dover edition by
Robert D. Mussey, Jr.

Manufactured in the United States of America
Dover Publications, Inc., 31 East 2nd Street,
Mineola, N.Y. 11501

Library of Congress Cataloging-in-Publication Data

Cabinet-maker's guide.
    The first American furniture finisher's manual.

    Reprint. Originally published: Concord, N.H. :
J.B. Moore, 1827. With new introd. and glossary.
    Bibliography: p.
    1. Furniture finishing.   I. Mussey, Robert D.
II. Title.
TT199.4.C33   1987   684.1′043   87-22246
ISBN 0-486-25530-1 (pbk.)

INTRODUCTION TO THE DOVER EDITION

The Gods hear men's hands before their lips,
And heed beyond all crying and sacrifice
Sight of things done and noise of laboring men.

Originally the art of fine furniture finishing was largely the private reserve of a select group of journeyman cabinetmakers, varnishmakers, and allied guild artisans. Great secrecy surrounded the true composition of varnish and stain formulations. The original guildbook of the painters', stainers', and varnishers' guild of York, England, gives us a glimpse of the exalted view that the guild held of itself and its knowledge as early as 1515. Titled *The Olde and Annciente Ordinances Articles and Customes or Mistery* [sic] *or Occupation of the Painters* . . . , it contains no written formulas, but devotes itself to the application of rules by which the guild's secrets were to be taught to apprentices and hidden from outsiders.

National jealousies developed, with French craftsmen competing to imitate "the best Italian" varnishes, the English formulating concoctions "to equal the best French varnishes," and everyone competing to surpass Chinese and Japanese lacquer work, which, periodically, had been the rage in Europe for centuries. By 1800, American craftsmen had entered the market in earnest and were vaunting their own ability to compete with more established European traditions. No vote was ever taken or a consensus established to declare a winner, but clearly many of the far-reaching claims indicate that they were all self-declared winners.

This spirited competition gave rise to contests sponsored by various national "philosophical societies," each offering sizeable prizes and inducements for discoveries of new and superior materials and formulas. These societies were usually governed by men of commerce and leaders of state, who hoped that local craftsmen would advance their national manufactures and industries to compete better in a world of increasingly international markets. But beyond such commercial interests, these leaders were trumpeting the superior vision, skill, and artistry of their own craftsmen over those of neighboring countries. They could display the "latest, most genteel fashions" in their homes and, thereby, their own overall superiority in taste, and perhaps in all matters.

Additional fuel for the fire of competition was supplied by the rise of the Age of Reason and with it the science of chemistry. Prior to this, alchemy and popular lore supplied the salient facts about the origins and true nature of pigments and resins. By the late eighteenth century, savants were unsatisfied with the considerable faith required to accept these previous sources of knowledge. The Age of Reason reverberated with minute researches into the true sources of plant resins, crude chemical experiments to discover their makeup, and highly controlled tests of their comparative virtues in prepared varnishes. Though the furnace of these extensive efforts did not yield dramatic, definitive new results until well into the nineteenth century, the fire was thus being stoked long before.

At the same time, far-reaching colonial explorations were providing supplies of new resins, dye plants, and pigments for these researches. Since one of the principal economic roots of colonialism was the need for such new materials, an important task assigned to early explorers was to locate, classify, and develop supplies of botanical and mineral resources. Hence artists and botanists were usually included among the voyagers. By 1650, the Americas were already well-developed sources of dyewoods to the Spanish, numerous resins to the French, and pine pitch to the English Navy.

Though furniture craftsmen continued to be bound by traditions of guild training and practice, the written record bears strong testament that they too had begun to experiment, constantly striving for artistic perfection. The rise of the "Age of Cabinetmaking" in the early eighteenth century in England and France resulted in explosive changes in construction, materials used, and complexity of design. New skills were required to execute daring new ideas. Preceded by relatively crude, heavy constructions and joinery derived from the traditions of housebuilding, new methods relied on careful use of lighter woods, sparer constructions, designs with elaborate curves and carving, and often the overlay of exciting veneers. These new designs were bold, ostentatious, and magnificent, and they demanded appropriately sassy finishes.

Finishes evolved from the uniformly dark, dull stains of Jacobean oak to brighter, more luminous colors. Stain and dye materials brought from around the world made this possible. Coatings changed from relatively easily applied linseed oil and beeswax, with their dull and easily harmed surfaces, to meticulously built-up coats of varnish, polished to perfection. These new finishes were formulated with plant resins and oils that, like the stains and dyes, were brought from around the world. Though the manufacture of the new varnishes drew on traditional guild knowledge, writings of the period reflect the constant detailed experimentation necessary to adapt the varnishes to new uses. This perpetual striving was then, and is now, at the heart of the furniture finisher's craft.

Given the powerful motivations and extensive labors of these diverse groups, it is not surprising that a considerable body of printed texts survives to document these efforts. But, unlike sources in other fine arts, these texts have rarely been studied, although comprehensive examination would illuminate the critical role that finishes have played in the aesthetics of furniture craftsmen. A careful comparative reading reveals that this finishing literature can be classed in several categories:

1. Papers presented to philosophical societies, such as the first accurate description of the manufacture and use of oriental lacquer. Titled "Mémoire sur le vernis de la Chine" ("Report on Chinese Lacquer"), it was presented to the French Academy of Sciences in 1704 by the widely traveled Jesuit priest Père D'Incarville.

2. Technical handbooks written primarily for the edification and amusement of the genteel dilettante, whose hobbies often included practice of various branches of the fine and applied arts. Of this type, the foremost is the widely known *A Treatise of Japanning and Varnishing* by Stalker and Parker (London, 1688). It is unknown how accurately the instructions in this classic mirror actual practices of the day, since they may have been simplified to be within the grasp of aristocratic students, whose success in learning was much to the advantage of the teacher. At the very least it provides a complete list of finishing materials available and a broad outline of procedures of the time.

3. Encyclopedias and dictionaries of the arts and sciences are an important source of a different kind. Those of

Rousseau and Diderot are prominent. The first widely printed in America was *Dobson's Encyclopaedia; or a Dictionary of Arts, Sciences* ... (Philadelphia, 1798), which includes extensive entries under "Varnishes," "Stains," "Resins," etc.

4. Treatises on varnishmaking and finishing materials, written primarily for manufacturers, scholars, chemists, and savants. They usually included specific formulations and directions for working craftsmen, but also strong theoretical components. Foremost of this genre is Watin's *L'Art du peintre, doreur, vernisseur* ("The Art of the Painter, Gilder, Varnisher"; Paris, 1769, and later editions). This is a treasurehouse of information about actual practices, materials, and formulas of the day. The author had worked for years as a manufacturer of varnishes, artists' pigments, and gilding supplies. His work includes accurate descriptions of all materials used during that period in Paris, along with notes on their sources and then-current prices.

Notable also among this group of books was one by Professor Tingry, a Geneva chemist. His *The Painter's and Varnisher's Guide* (Geneva, 1803; London, 1804; Philadelphia, 1831; and other editions) represented a milestone effort by a practical chemist to understand the chemical nature of the materials and processes of varnishmaking.

Also important in this class of sources are works by A. Tripier-Deveux, *Traité théorique et pratique sur l'art de faire les vernis* (Paris: L. Mathias, 1845), and Jules Henri Violette, *Guide pratique de la fabrication des vernis* (Paris, 1866). Both authors were working manufacturers; thus the information is reflective of actual practice.

5. Specialty publications for working tradesmen, such as *Genuine Receipt for making the Famous Vernis Martin; or, as it is called by the English, Martin's Copal Varnish* ... (Paris and Dublin: W. Wilson, 1776). The anonymous author claims

to reveal the much sought-after varnish formulation of several brothers who were master varnishers to the French court and whose work was widely admired. The methods and materials described for making a hard copal-and-oil varnish would have been of interest only to the most skilled of working craftsmen, as the methods required highly specialized and detailed procedures. However, it accurately reflects methods used at that time for such varnishes.

6. Cabinetmakers' pattern books and dictionaries were another source of information. While Thomas Sheraton's *Cabinet Dictionary* (London, 1803) attempted to educate cabinetmakers on the whole range of furniture and upholstery details and their classical foundations, valuable information about finishing materials and methods was interspersed. Sheraton's intimate connection with various branches of the trade and numerous working craftsmen makes this a valuable source of historical information.

By universal agreement, Jacques André Roubo's *L'Art du menuisier* ("The Art of the Woodworker"; 3 vols., Paris, 1769–74) is the greatest work of any age or country on cabinetmaking in its various branches. It includes an extensive section on furniture-finishing methods, materials, and tools. Roubo had intimate associations with the trade and his information is considered highly reliable. The claims of authors of certain other such technical dictionaries are questionable. Most dictionary compilers stated they consulted the "best sources extant," but close-mouthed craftsmen with trade secrets to protect may well not have been among those sources.

7. Artists' and tradesmen's guidebooks and recipe books comprise the last and largest category of printed historical sources. Hundreds of these titles are known to survive. Sometimes they were compiled by artisans, more often by publishers with the help of presumably experienced work-

ing craftsmen. Commonly the formulas and directions were lifted verbatim or hastily paraphrased from other such guidebooks, so that it can be difficult to trace material back to its original source. The titles changed, and each volume was republished with assurances that this was the first time that hitherto secret information was available to the artisan. This shameless publishing practice predated effective copyright laws and was hidden from detection in translations from original sources in other languages and when the sources cited were merely "the best authorities and craftsmen now working." So for example we find that *Secrets concernant les arts et métiers*, first published in Paris in 1716, was subsequently republished in original and augmented versions in four languages in at least fourteen cities in five countries in at least 24 editions over the following 125 years. This wide acceptance, however, testifies strongly to actual use by craftsmen of some of the directions, and the information can probably be relied on as largely reflective of actual historic practices. The present volume, *The Cabinet-Maker's Guide*, fits within this large class of practical guidebooks and follows the same pattern of numerous reprintings and appropriation by other publishers without attribution.

A wide variety of such artisans' guide- and formula books can be found. Some were limited to specialized, narrowly defined topics such as oil painting or varnishmaking. Others covered a whole panoply of miscellaneous recipes for craftsmen of every conceivable trade. Despite differences, they were generally oriented toward the working craftsman.

By 1800, however, profound social, economic, and technological changes had occurred in America, creating a new class of craftsman with new needs. These new needs eventually led to fundamental changes in the practical guidebooks. The closed-guild system had begun to break down, and a series of labor strikes caused an upheaval among

Philadelphia cabinetmakers. Swarms of new immigrants were available to the labor market, and manufacturers often circumvented the union rules and hired labor with less than traditional training at less than union price-book rates. With a growing merchant fleet and enough capital to set up large manufactories that could satisfy both burgeoning domestic needs and international export markets, ways were sought to train labor that did not require the traditional extended period of apprenticeship before a man could perform skilled labor for hire.

In the first quarter of the nineteenth century, both native-born and immigrant Americans began to spread rapidly inland from the Eastern seaboard and ply their trades away from the established economies of major cities. As they moved away from urban centers, they no longer had ready access to supplies of manufactured materials from London. In the already very specialized organization of the cabinet-making trade in Boston, one man was sawyer, another joiner, another carver, another upholsterer, another finisher. In rural New England, Kentucky, or Ohio, newly arrived cabinetmakers had to practice all these skills, including making their own finishing materials, such as stains and varnishes, and repairing damaged gilding and false graining. A new need was established that was not served by the traditional printed sources of directions for practicing these skills.

The peculiar nature of American democracy also disposed craftsmen to rebel against the harsh nature of the traditional training system, and to believe that they could learn and practice the rarified skills of cabinetmaking and finishing by themselves without the constant tutelage of an overlord master. And through the agency of the printing press and mass publishing, it was finally possible for Everyman to be his own master and self-teacher of the traditional secrets and skills essential to the trades. As the United States developed its new independent identity, the thirst for knowledge among its citizens was voracious. And small publishers rushed to quench this thirst.

Our *Cabinet-Maker's Guide* was designed exactly for this new series of needs. My research leads me to conclude that it was the first book printed in America to deal exclusively with furniture finishing. In the Preface to the "Weber" edition of 1809, the author expresses his wish that the volume "will be particularly convenient to country manufacturers, who have not the convenience of [an urban] market." It was not designed for the high-style urban cabinetmaker with all the support of urban specialization. "In London it is hardly worth while to make varnish, unless in large quantities, as there are several shops where it may be had very good, and at a fair price; but in the country, where the carraige [sic] is an object, and you cannot depend upon the genuineness of the article, it is necessary to be known by the practical mechanic" (*The Cabinet-Maker's Guide*, 1827 ed., p. 32).

The significance of *The Cabinet-Maker's Guide* lies not in any dramatically new varnish formulas or working methods. In fact, most of the formulas given fall within one class of varnishes, those called in the period "spirit varnishes." These required dissolving a resin or mixture of resins in ethyl alcohol, generally termed at that time "spirits of wine." Spirit varnishes were among the easiest types of varnishes to be made in the small shop, requiring a minimum of equipment and knowledge. They were already widely known as traditional furniture varnishes.

Nor are the formulas and materials for stains significantly different from what had been appearing in similar artisans' recipe books for the previous 150 years. Brazilwood, logwood, French berries, archil, and barberry root had all been used extensively by the time of the first publication of our text in the United States. Further, we know from Rufus Porter's *A Select Collection of Valuable and Curious Arts* (Concord, N.H.: Jacob B. Moore, 1825) that about ninety percent of the raw materials called for in recipes in *The Cabinet-Maker's Guide* were available for sale in Boston at "135 Washington Street." Porter conveniently lists the then-current prices, allowing us to see clearly that materials required in our *Guide* were among the less expensive finishing materials available on the market. The modest price of materials called for in its recipes made the book particularly well suited to its stated market.

In order to reach an even broader audience, the first American publisher, Ansel Phelps of Greenfield, Massachusetts, advertised his new offering in a newspaper he also published: "Just published. . . . The Cabinet-Maker's Guide. . . . This work is also interesting to the housewife, containing some valuable information in reference to certain branches of domestic economy—but it is particularly so to the cabinetmaker, the Chair Maker, Painter and other artists. . . . and will be found to contain many new and valuable receipts for giving that elegance and finish which distinguishes the best European work, and which will enable the American to compete with the English artist."[1] The price of this volume was 50 cents, the same as a quart of alcohol for varnishes in the Boston of 1825 (a pound of shellac resin then cost 96 cents). All craftsmen, no matter what their location or how successful they were, could easily afford this modest price.

Our text was thus well designed to strike a democratic chord in America. It was not dramatically original, it did not require extremely specialized apparatus, it was inexpensive. It was, in fact, the first ideal "Everyman's furniture-finish-

---

[1]*The Franklin Herald and Public Advertiser* (Greenfield, Mass.), Nov. 1, 1825, Vol. XXXIV, No. 769, p. 3.

ing guidebook." The veil had been lifted from the "Annciente
. . . Customes or Mistery," and this guidebook would become
far more successful and widely accepted than the original
author and publisher could ever have dreamed.

The first edition of *The Cabinet-Maker's Guide* that is
definitely known to exist appeared in London in 1809
(published by John Arliss), a slim pamphlet of 36 pages in
paper wrappers. The author is given as "Peter Weber,
Cabinet-Maker and Ebonist," though my research has not
located his name among those of cabinetmakers then working in London. This 1809 edition is labeled "Second Edition."
Several antiquarians familiar with such guidebooks have
suggested that no "First Edition" ever existed, that in fact
the Weber edition was the first. By this interpretation,
labeling the book "Second Edition" made it appear to enjoy a
wide popularity, thus promoting sales. This conjecture,
however, remains mere speculation, unless a volume labeled
"First Edition" should turn up to prove the contrary.

Following the 1809 edition, an 1818 (date uncertain)
edition appeared. This was merely a rewording of the
previous edition with some miscellaneous recipes added, and
the author was now "Thomas Howard." Apparently this also
sold well, because in 1825 two new London editions appeared,
greatly expanded from the original 36 pages to 223 pages in
one case and 108 pages in the other. These were two different
publishers, each claiming original authorship! They were
followed closely by the first American edition, published also
in 1825 (by Ansel Phelps of Greenfield, Massachusetts) and
based on the shorter of the two London editions of the same
year. A second American edition, identical with the Phelps
text, was published in 1827 by Jacob B. Moore in Concord,
New Hampshire. This is the edition reprinted in the present
volume. Another London edition appeared in 1837 (some
catalogs wrongly state 1830 on the basis of the date on an
engraving), this time credited to one "G. A. Siddons."

Further English editions followed in 1875 and 1897 and a Spanish edition in 1925, all of which were expansions and alterations of the 1825 versions.

This was not the end by any means. The traditional practice of piracy without attribution appears to have reached a zenith with *The Cabinet-Maker's Guide* in nineteenth-century America. *The Painter, Gilder, and Varnisher's Companion* (Philadelphia: H. C. Baird, 1850) reprinted many of the formulas verbatim with no credit given. This title alone was republished at least eighteen times with changes and additions. Other works based partially or wholly on our *Cabinet-Maker's Guide* include *The Cabinet-Maker and Upholsterer's Companion* by J. Stokes (Philadelphia: H. C. Baird, 1852), also reprinted many times. I have located over fifty distinct titles of the nineteenth and early twentieth centuries that include parts of our volume, either copied exactly or closely paraphrased. By the end of this period, it is certain that publishers had no idea of the origins or the original author of the material. In discussing this material, therefore, it generally means little to refer to specific editions; in most cases we must be satisfied to speak vaguely of "the text."

It is fair to attach great significance to this text. In one form or another, hundreds of thousands of copies of many of the recipes and directions were in the hands of working craftsmen all over the Eastern United States and in other countries. Though we cannot definitely trace the application of any of the formulations to any single specific piece of furniture, we may assume that the text accurately depicts actual use on many pieces of nineteenth-century furniture.

Some of the recipes and methods continue to be followed almost identically today in many museum and private restoration workshops. While this reflects the strong resistance to change and the reliance upon old traditions that persist even today, it also suggests the utility of the actual

preparations and the universal and practical chord struck by
The Cabinet-Maker's Guide. Besides having been the vehicle
of so many practical, successful, and accessible methods of
the previous 125 years, the text also made important and
original contributions to certain aspects of finishing history.
It contains the first mention I have found of French polishing
as a technique of varnish application, and of French polish as
a material for varnishing. The 1809 and 1818 editions make
no mention of these. However, all of the 1825 and later
editions cited above, including the one reprinted here, state:
"The method of varnishing furniture, by means of *rubbing*
it on the surface of the wood, is of comparatively modern
date, though bees'-wax has been used either by itself, or
mixed with spirits of turpentine for a very considerable
period . . . ." Extensive directions are then given for the very
tricky and laborious method of French polishing or "friction
varnishing." The method is remarkably similar to that used
today by many restorers and finishers.

We also find the first known mention of the production of
"glass-paper," a precursor of today's sandpaper. The method
given calls for pounding up glass into fine particles, sifting
them to uniform particle size, and gluing them to a type of
heavy paper.

A rare description of the then-common method of finishing
off the wood in preparation for varnishing or polishing is
afterward detailed. This method follows closely the French
method explained by Roubo in *L'Art du menuisier.* A solid
block of pumice stone was ground flat, the wood was wet
down with water to raise the rough grain, then rubbed with
this stone to cut off the whiskers of raised grain. The method
aided in filling in open grain pores, as the process created a
"sludge" of wood pulp and water which the rubbing packed
into the open pores. And it compacted and hardened the
surface prior to final finishing and polishing operations.

The "author" of *The Cabinet-Maker's Guide* also distin-

guishes between staining and dyeing, the first such distinc-
tion I know of in an American source. He discusses the
serious problems related to the fading of dyes and stains used
at that time, and how these problems led cabinetmakers to
discontinue their use for a while. He also includes a description of a dyeing trough or "chair-maker's copper," also the
first such description I know of.

In a clearer picture than previously available, he describes
implements useful to the manufacture and application of
varnishes. The "sand bath" and "varnish pot" referred to by
the author were used to heat the resins to dissolve them more
completely and to keep the varnish warm for brush application. This resulted in a better flowout on the wood surfaces.

A careful reading of *The Cabinet-Maker's Guide* also
elucidates the complex, ambiguous meaning of the word
"polishing." In the early nineteenth century, "polishing"
encompassed a broad range of meanings, unlike today. It
could mean burnishing the wood with a block of pumice stone
(as just described) prior to other finishing operations. It
could mean following this by rubbing the raw wood, slowly
and laboriously, with a mixture of the powdered abrasive
Tripoli and linseed oil till a bright shine developed. It could
mean developing a glossy finish by rubbing beeswax or a
beeswax-turpentine paste onto the raw wood. Or polishing
could also refer to the leveling of varnishes by means of
abrasives in water, usually applied with cotton flannel
wrapped around a cork block or a tightly rolled wad of cloth.
By this method, the rubbing continued until all brush marks,
dust, and surface irregularities were rubbed out with the
fine abrasive paste and a fine gloss was brought up. And last,
polishing could refer to French polishing, in which a special
varnish was applied laboriously with a wad of cloth instead
of a brush. The procedure was continued until a glorious
bright gloss was achieved. Today, polishing generally refers

only to an application and buffing of a paste wax or oil emulsion over an existing varnish or finish to improve its appearance.

In keeping with the author's stated intention of providing cabinetmakers with instructions and recipes for a broad range of miscellaneous finishing arts, the book contains a real grab bag of these. Instructions for gilding, mirror silvering, cleaning marble, making bronzing paints, making Boulle-work marquetry, and other miscellaneous arts supply information ample enough to remedy deficiencies in the skills of any cabinetmaker. After this broad-ranging review, we are left to wonder if there could possibly be any other subjects a finisher would need to know about.

In the Introduction, the author touts at length the merits of the book, claiming that "The CABINET-MAKER'S GUIDE is, perhaps, the only work tha[t] may be properly called a Manual of the Art, and the rapid sale which it met with, is a proof of the estimation in which it was held [in previous editions]." Though this piece of puffery is common to every tradesman's manual of the period, the publication of fourteen known editions and seventy-plus pirated texts amply testifies to the ultimate truth of the assertion. *The Cabinet-Maker's Guide* cut broadly across the spectrum of successful recipes and practices of the previous century while at the same time striking the great chord of democracy in a new and developing country.

Students of furniture and finishing history should find this an invaluable source for interpretation of our antique-furniture heritage.

ROBERT D. MUSSEY, JR.

Society for the Preservation of
  New England Antiquities
Boston, 1987

Special thanks to Mr. Brock Jobe for his help and encouragement in researching this material.

The following libraries, archives, and private booksellers provided invaluable assistance in preparation of this text: The Baker Library of the Harvard Business School, Cambridge, Mass.; The Society for the Preservation of New England Antiquities, Boston; The Essex Institute, Salem, Mass.; The American Antiquarian Society, Worcester, Mass.; The Massachusetts Historical Society, Boston; The Rhode Island Historical Society, Providence; The New York Public Library, New York; The Winterthur Museum, Winterthur, Del.; The Library of Congress, Washington; The Boston Public Library, Boston; Charles B. Wood III, Antiquarian Bookseller, Boston.

GLOSSARY OF TERMS

Air-wood: Normally, air-dried wood. In its context on page 53, the term seems to refer to a particular variety of wood, the identity of which is now obscure.

Alkanet root: A traditional organic dye material yielding a strong though fairly fugitive red. A Southeastern U.S. plant, *Alkanna tinctoria (Anchusa tinctoria)*, was a source, though related English and French plants had long been used for a similar dye.

Aloes: A bitter, purgative, yellow-colored juice expressed from several species of plants of the lily family, particularly *Aloe barbadensis* (formerly called *Aloe vera*). Formerly used as a drug.

Alum: A whitish transparent mineral salt, chemically a double sulfate of aluminum and potassium.

Amber: A hard fossilized resin, traditionally mined or washed up on the shores of lakes, and, especially, the Baltic Sea. It is not soluble in ethyl alcohol, and it generally had to be liquified or "run" at high temperature, cooled, and then dissolved in an extremely hot drying oil, such as linseed oil. The necessary high temperature made the mixture explosive and extremely dangerous for the small workman to produce. It is doubtful, however, that the author of *The Cabinet-*

Maker's Guide can be referring to real amber resin, as his directions for solution do not call for the high temperature and elaborate process required at that time.

Aquafortis: Concentrated nitric acid.

Archil (orchil): A dye or stain derived from a lichen *(Rocella)* that grows on rocks on the shore of the Mediterranean, in the Canary and Cape Verde Islands, and elsewhere. It yields a rich purple color, beautiful but not durable. It was made by soaking the lichen in an alkali over a period of time, after which the mixture took on a purplish red color. Treated with additional alkali, the color could be turned into blue. Litmus was manufactured by similar means from the same or similar lichens.

Barberry: One of a number of shrubs (especially *Berberis vulgaris*) common in English and American hedge borders. The bark and roots dye a fine yellow.

Black lead: Natural graphite of the kind used in lead pencils; often called "plumbago" in period texts.

Boiled linseed oil: *See* Linseed oil.

Boll ammoniac: Corruption of "Bole Armoniac" or "Armenian bole," a soft, colored, friable natural earth traditionally used in the ground coats of gilding.

Box: Boxwood.

Brazil dust: Sawdust of the Brazilwood tree (any of a number of species of trees of the family Leguminosae, found in Brazil, elsewhere in tropical America, and in Southeast Asia). A very heavy wood of glowing red color, used for red and purple dyes. An item of enormous importance in the seventeenth- and eighteenth-century dye trade.

Brick-dust: Powdered brick, sometimes used by cabinet-makers to fill the open grain of mahogany prior to varnishing and polishing operations. Mixed with linseed oil, it also formed a paste or "sludge" for polishing woods.

Brown ochre: *See* Ochre.

Brown spirit varnish: Probably a relatively cheap common varnish made with rosin and turpentine.

Burgundy pitch: A varnish resin derived from the Norway spruce *(Picea abies).*

Burnt sienna: *See* Sienna.

Burnt umber: *See* Umber.

Butter of antimony: Deliquescent antimony trichloride, a caustic anhydrous chloride.

Call (hot board): Today usually spelled "caul." A shaped wooden form used in gluing down veneer to distribute pressure evenly over the entire veneer surface.

Cement: *See* the section on "Cements," pages 82–84.

Chair-maker's copper: Copper trough then used by chairmakers to soak wood to make it pliable for bending into curved chair parts.

Cochineal: A natural organic dyestuff made from the dried bodies of the females of the insect *Dactylopius coccus (Coccus cacti)*, which lives on various cactus plants in Mexico and Central America. The extracted pigment is called carmine.

Copal: One of a large group of resins of similar properties but derived from unrelated species of trees and sometimes gathered from the ground in fossilized form. Some copals are extremely hard, such as the fossil New Zealand kauri copal and the various African copals; these formed the basis of hard oleoresinous varnishes from 1840 until the advent of synthetic resins in the twentieth century. The soft copals are alcohol-soluble, and undoubtedly one of these is meant by the author here, possibly Manila copal, from *Agathis Dammara.* Other alcohol-soluble copals were known from the Far East, Africa, and South America.

Copperas: An iron sulfate; originally this term denoted blue vitriol (a hydrated copper sulfate), later sometimes the entire class of metal sulfates.

Currier's shavings: Small pieces and trimmings of leather, waste from various branches of the leatherworking trades.

Drachm (dram): 27⅓ grains or ⅟₁₆ ounce, avoirdupois weight.

Dragon's blood: Originally, a dark red resin from the stems of some species of *Dracaena* (Agavaceae) of the Old World tropics. Now dragon's blood is more commonly from species of *Daemonorops* (Palmae), grown in East Africa. In all of its varieties, dragon's blood is alcohol-soluble and has long been used to tint varnishes.

Drugget: A coarse woolen cloth used for floor coverings, tablecloths, etc.

Dutch metal: A pigment of varying composition, made from powdered bronze or brass reacted with various chemicals to give goldlike colors of all different hues. Dutch metal was also made in leaf form as an imitation of gold leaf. See page 62 of the text.

Dying: Now (and usually in the nineteenth century as well) spelled "dyeing." The process of coloring wood veneers throughout their thickness by soaking them and boiling them in a vat of dye. This was done prior to cutting to shape and gluing to furniture grounds.

Elder coal: Fine powdered charcoal made from elder wood and used at that time for polishing. Its fairly high proportion of oily matter aided in bringing up a gloss.

Flake white: A white-lead pigment (a form of lead oxide) widely used in painting since antiquity and still the finest white pigment through the early nineteenth century.

French berries (Avignon berries): The fruit of the French plant *Rhamnus infectoria* (found also elsewhere from South Europe to Iran), smaller in size than peas and yielding a yellow dye.

Gamboge: A yellow gum resin (mixture of a gum and a resin) produced by several species of trees of the genus

Garcinia, indigenous to India, Ceylon, and Southeast Asia. It was used in watercolors, spirit varnishes, and gold lacquer.

Genoa soap: "White soda soap in a less pure state is called Genoa soap."—*Penny Cyclopedia*, London, 1842.

Gill: One-quarter pint, liquid measure.

Gold size: A thin adhesive coating of high quality, used as a glue to hold leaves of gold leaf or silver leaf on the ground.

Grain tin: Powdered tin or tin filings.

Green copperas: *See* Copperas.

Gum anime (anime, gum animae, gum aulmae): A resin, but like many resins improperly labeled a gum at that time. Considerable confusion still remains about the origin and nature of anime. According to some American authors, it was of South American origin; some European authors speak of "American" origin. Twentieth-century sources, however, claim that it was one of the East African soft copals. In fact the name "gum anime" was probably applied indiscriminately to a number of resins from different sources. Apparently they all, or nearly all, had in common the properties of being relatively soft, clear, and alcohol soluble. The names "Zanzibar copal" and "Zanzibar anime" were often applied to what was presumably the East African anime.

Gum arabic: A gum tapped from any of several species of acacia trees, particularly *Acacia Senegal* of West Africa. Water-soluble, traditionally used as a binder and medium in certain types of watercolor painting and as a gold size.

Gum Benjamin: *See* Gum benzoin.

Gum benzoin (Gum Benjamin): A dark, distinctively aromatic balsamic resin from various trees of the genus *Styrax* of Southeast Asia. Used at least as early as the seventeenth century as a principal resin in varnishes, later as a plasticizing resin in varnishes, and in the nineteenth and twentieth centuries in French polishing to create a final glaze of intensely high gloss.

Gum guaicum (guaiac, guaiacum, gum guaiacum): A resin of a greenish cast, much used in medicine. Derived from the lignum-vitae tree of tropical America, actually two species of trees, *Guaiacum officinale* and *Guaiacum sanctum.*

Gum lac (lac): Lac, the basis of shellac and seed lac, is a resinous secretion deposited on certain trees in the Far East by a small scale insect, *Laccifer lacca.* When gathered from the trees, lac includes considerable dirt, insect bodies, and sticks; it is called "stick lac" in this form. When lac is washed, melted, filtered through coarse cloth, stretched out to a thin sheet, cooled, and broken into small pieces, it is called "shellac" (originally "shell-lac"). (What is nowadays sold as shellac is a solution of the resin shellac in alcohol.) Another processed form, in small grains, is called "seed lac." The resin is available in several different natural colors and purities, and it can be further purified by extracting the natural wax with solvents, or bleached to make it perfectly clear. Lac was widely available in Europe in some forms since the seventeenth century and in America at least since the early nineteenth century. It has formed the basis of most French polishes.

Gum mastic (mastic): A resin derived from the shrub *Pistacia Lentiscus.* This relative of the pistachio tree is found all around the Mediterranean, but commercial production of mastic is almost exclusively confined to the Greek island of Chios. It has been used from ancient times, chiefly in varnishes for oil paintings but to a lesser extent in furniture varnishes.

Gum sandrach (sandarac): A resin from *Tetraclinis articulata,* a North African tree of the cypress family. In the past it may have been confused with resins derived from junipers. Sandarac is alcohol-soluble, giving a clear, hard, "white" varnish, formerly commonly used on furniture when a nearly colorless varnish was desired.

Hispaniola: Cuban mahogany, an extremely dense, dark, highly figured cabinet wood, favored in the seventeenth through the nineteenth century. It is now unavailable because of overcutting and altered trading patterns.

Hot board: *See* Call.

Indian red: A variety of natural iron oxide imported from India, varying in color from light to deep purple-red. The term is now used for an artificial red iron oxide of a somewhat different composition.

Indigo: A blue vegetable dye used for coloring fabrics and as a paint pigment. The dye is yielded by different plants of the genus *Indigofera*, the principal source in the early nineteenth century probably being *Indigofera tinctoria*, of Indian origin.

Isinglass: A pure fish gelatin or glue, derived principally from the sturgeon.

Japanning: A decorative finishing method common to the eighteenth and nineteenth centuries, generally employing paint pigments mixed with shellac varnish as a medium. It was a European imitation of Oriental lacquer work. When worked on furniture, multiple ground coats, usually of chalk and binder, were applied to seal the wood and provide a smooth base for the decorative painting applied over it. Exact methods and materials varied over time and from one country to another.

King's yellow: A refined form of orpiment (*see also* Orpiment).

Lacker: Lacquer. See pages 75 through 77.

Lake: A generic term meaning a transparent or translucent pigment produced by precipitating an organic dye or coloring matter on an inert base such as calcium sulfate or aluminum hydrate. The name is ultimately a derivative of "lac," which in its raw form contains a large quantity of natural red dye. Eventually the term came to signify any pigment, usually a red one, derived by the foregoing method.

Lake was often used by artists as a thin glaze over layers of paint to shade them.

Lamp-black: Nearly pure amorphous carbon collected in brick chambers from the incomplete combustion of tar, pitch, or resin. Not true black, but slightly bluish in color.

Linseed oil: A natural drying oil expressed from flaxseed. Before the adoption of synthetic vehicles, it formed the basis of most oil paints and oil-based varnishes. It can be heated with any of several metallic oxides to improve its drying properties; when so treated it is called "boiled" linseed oil. Linseed oil has been used since ancient times by itself as a finish for wood, although when so used as a furniture finish it is liable to injury.

Litharge (massicot): The yellow monoxide of lead, formed by the gentle roasting of white lead. Used as a pigment and as a drier in paints and varnishes. Its color can range to orangish.

Logwood (Campeche wood): A hard, heavy wood from a tree *(Haematoxylum campechianum)* native to the Bay of Campeche region of Mexico, Honduras, and parts of the West Indies. Yields a red dye which, used with various mordants, can produce brown, black, and blue colors as well. Now supplanted by synthetics.

Lunar caustic: Fused silver nitrate.

Mineral green (mountain green): A green pigment made from the mineral malachite, chemically a basic copper carbonate. Much used in painting from ancient times to about 1800, when it was replaced by various artificial green pigments.

Muller and stone (muller and grindstone, muller and grinding slab): Stone implements traditionally used for grinding paint pigments. Typically the stone was a rectangular slab of granite or marble, eighteen inches square, ground dead flat on its top surface. The pigment in oil or other vehicle was placed on the stone and pulverized to a uniform consistency using the muller, which was usually an egg-shaped piece of granite about three inches in diameter and five inches long with the large end of the "egg" ground off to a flat surface, which was rubbed against the grindstone.

Nut galls: A nut gall is a small, leathery sphere formed as an insect case on various oak trees. Rich in tannic acid, nut galls were traditionally used in combination with other materials to form a rich brown or yellow-brown dye.

Nut oil (walnut oil): A drying oil expressed from walnuts, traditionally used by artists and varnishmakers for the finest clear "white" (colorless) varnishes and as a paint medium where the color of the oil would not alter that of the pigment.

Ochre: A class of natural earth pigments consisting of silica, clay, and iron oxides. The presence of different iron oxides in various hydrous or anhydrous forms produces different colors, including red, brown, and yellow varieties. *See also* Spruce ochre.

Oil of vitriol (vitriol): Sulfuric acid.

Orpiment: A yellow pigment prepared from the mineral arsenic trisulfide. A refined form was called "king's yellow." It was highly poisonous and destroyed the color of other pigments it came in contact with, so it fell into disuse.

Patent yellow: Lead oxychloride. A bright and permanent yellow pigment widely used from 1790 to 1830 because it was not as dangerous to use as king's yellow.

Patteras (pateras): The plural of patera is properly "paterae." A patera is a classical Greek element of decoration, in furniture usually a circular or oval decorative veneer inlay. The name is also applied to a similar circular applied carved decoration, often with formalized leaves or flowers.

Pearlash (pearl ash): Potash.

Pipkin: A type of small ceramic or metal container.

Poppy oil (poppyseed oil): A natural light drying oil

expressed from the seeds of the opium poppy, *Papaver somniferum*. Traditionally used as a paint medium, especially with certain paint pigments, which are not appreciably darkened by the clear, very light-colored oil. Also used as the basis for some artists' varnishes where extreme clarity and lightness of color are desired.

Prussian blue (Paris blue, Berlin blue): The first modern synthetic pigment, first produced in Berlin in or about 1704. Chemically, ferric ferrocyanide or a similar compound; of a deep blue color.

Pumice-stone: A soft, porous rock of volcanic origin, ground and used as a powdered abrasive or flattened and used as a rubbing or polishing block to smooth flat surfaces of wood. Used also for flattening and smoothing irregularities in coats of varnish before recoating.

Putty powder: Tin oxide or a mixture of tin oxide and lead oxide, used for polishing.

Quick-lime: Calcium oxide.

Quicksilver: Mercury.

Quirk: A small, acute hollow in certain wood moldings.

Raw sienna: *See* Sienna.

Red-lead (minium): The red tetroxide of lead, made by heating white lead. Used traditionally by painters as a red pigment, and as an oxidizer added to linseed oil and varnishes to make them dry more rapidly.

Red ochre: *See* Ochre.

Rose pink: A lake, generally made by precipitating the red dye from brazilwood onto whiting or chalk.

Rosin (colophony): A resin derived from any of several conifers, particularly pine, spruce, and fir. Traditionally, when the raw sap was gathered in containers, it was often called "turpentine." When this was burned, it yielded a black, gummy "pitch" valued by navies for ship caulking. When distilled, the sap yielded fluid "spirits of turpentine" (what is now usually referred to simply as "turpentine") and the resin called "rosin." Rosin continues to be manufactured by a similar process.

Rotten stone (rottenstone): A decomposed siliceous limestone, ground to a fine powder and used for fine polishing.

Ruddle: Red ochre (*see* Ochre).

Saffron: The golden yellow coloring matter that is extracted from the dried stigmas of the crocus flower, particularly *Crocus sativus.* Widely used also in cooking.

Sal-almoniac (sal ammoniac): Ammonium chloride.

Salt of tartar: Potassium carbonate.

Sap green: A light green pigment prepared from the juice of the ripe berries of the buckthorn *(Rhamnus cathartica);* a very fugitive substance.

Satin-wood: Wood from the Indian tree *Chloroxylon Swietenia* or certain similar West Indian trees, widely favored by English cabinetmakers at the end of the eighteenth and beginning of the nineteenth century because of its luminescent, satinlike appearance.

Scraping: In preparing wood for staining and polishing, specially sharpened steel scrapers were used to level minor high spots and imperfections, level veneer inlays to a uniform plane, and cut off stringy or raised grain. A scraped surface was true and smooth enough for further finishing operations.

Sienna: A class of earth pigments chemically similar to the ochres. Raw sienna is a brownish yellow. When heated it forms burnt sienna, with a warmer, reddish brown color.

Silver lace: Wire coated with silver and woven into lace.

Size: A very thin, watered-down mixture of glue, used as an initial sealer coat on wood and paper surfaces to prevent further coats of finish from soaking in too much. Size could be prepared from any of the animal glues.

Soap lees: Spent soap lye, an alkaline fluid derived in the soap-making process.

Spirits of salts: Muriatic (hydrochloric) acid.

Spirits of turpentine: A pungent, volatile, oily distillate of oleoresins obtained from various species of conifers. Identical with the liquid today usually called simply "turpentine."

Spirits of wine: Ethyl alcohol derived by distillation of wine or other alcoholic beverage. At that time spirits of wine evidently contained a fairly large proportion of water; often it was redistilled for varnishmaking and then called "rectified" spirits of wine.

Spruce ochre: A dark variety of yellow ochre (*see* Ochre).

Staining: The process of coloring wood in a completed piece of furniture. Usually a liquid is applied with a brush or rag, then the excess wiped off.

Sugar candy: Sugar clarified and purified by slow evaporation into a fine white crystalline form; a name for what we know today as fine white table sugar.

Sweet oil: Olive oil.

Tartar: A deposit left on the sides of wine casks in the process of fermentation of grapes, consisting chiefly of cream of tartar (potassium hydrogen tartrate). Still often used to polish metals.

Tooth-plane: A cabinetmaker's plane used in traditional veneer work. The plane iron is corrugated with small "teeth" in the cutting edge; the plane is used to roughen or "tooth" the wood ground to provide a better gluing surface for veneer. It was also used for the initial planing of cabinet woods with curly or tricky grain to prevent chips and tears in the wild grain. This was followed by scraping to present a smooth finish for final polishing.

Tripoli: A siliceous rock of variable composition (once thought to contain diatomaceous remains), ground to a fine powder and used for fine polishing.

Tumerick (turmeric): The powdered aromatic and pungent rhizomes of the Indian and Indonesian plant *Curcuma longa*, used to produce a yellow dye and as a major ingredient of curry.

Tunbridge ware: A form of nineteenth-century decorative veneer work, originating in the fashionable resort town of Tunbridge Wells, Kent, England. Slender strips of naturally colored woods of constrasting color were inlaid in intricate mosaiclike patterns. This work was applied to boxes, tea caddies, trays, and some furniture.

Umber: A class of natural brown earth pigments similar to the ochres and siennas but containing also manganese dioxide. Raw umber is a rather cold brown; when heated it forms burnt umber, with a warmer reddish brown color.

Vandyke brown (Van Dyke brown, Cassel earth, Cologne earth): A brown pigment derived from peat or similar organic substances.

Veneering hammer: A specialized cabinetmaker's tool used for pressing down veneer during gluing. It is shaped like a mallet with a flattened head, which usually has a rounded brass strip let in to distribute pressure and reduce friction and to prevent the hammer from gumming up with hot glue. A photograph of this tool may be found in *Practical Veneering* by Charles Hayward (London: Evans Bros., 1965), page 30.

Verdigris: A blue-green pigment known since ancient times. An acetate of copper, sometimes also copper carbonate or other products of the corrosion of copper, brass, or bronze.

Verditer: An inexpensive green pigment made from copper dissolved in nitric acid and precipitated on chalk.

Verjuice: The acid juice of green or unripe grapes, crab apples, or other sour fruit, expressed into a liquor, formerly much used in cooking.

Vermillion (vermilion, cinnabar): Red mercuric sulfide,

found in nature as the mineral cinnabar. In ancient times, cinnabar was crushed and ground for use as a red pigment. From an early date, however, it was also known how to combine the elements mercury and sulfur to make artificial vermilion.

Vitriolated indigo: The "solution of indigo in vitriol" mentioned on page 16.

Whiting: One form of natural calcium carbonate, used in powdered form for polishing.

Yellow ochre: *See* Ochre.

Sources Used in Preparation of Glossary

Adrosko, Rita J. *Natural Dyes in the United States.* 1968. Reprinted as *Natural Dyes and Home Dyeing.* New York: Dover, 1971.

Bailey, Liberty Hyde, et al. *Hortus Third: A Concise Dictionary of Plants Cultivated in the United States and Canada.* New York: Macmillan, 1976.

Barry, T. Hedley, et al. *The Chemistry of the Natural and Synthetic Resins.* London: Ernst Benn, 1926.

Boger, L. A., and Boger, H. B. *The Dictionary of Antiques and the Decorative Arts.* New York: Scribner's, 1967.

Bottler, Max, and Sabin, Alvah Horton. *German and American Varnishmaking.* New York: Wiley, 1912.

Brachert, Thomas. "Historische Klarlacke and Möbelpolituren." In 5 parts. *Maltechnik-Restauro* (Munich) (1978) nos. 1–4, pp. 56–65, 120–25, 185–93, 263–74; (1979) no. 2, pp. 132–34.

Brady, G. S., and Clauser, H. *Materials Handbook.* 11th ed. New York: McGraw-Hill, 1977.

Carroll, Charles. *The Timber Economy of Puritan New England*. Providence, R.I.: Brown Univ. Press, 1973.

Chatfield, H. W. *Varnish Constituents*. London: Leonard Hill, 1947.

Eklund, Jon. *The Incompleat Chymist . . . With a Dictionary of Obsolete Chemical Terms of the Period*. Smithsonian Studies in History and Technology no. 33. Washington, D.C.: Smithsonian Institution Press, 1973.

Encyclopædia Britannica. 15th ed.

Gettens, Rutherford J., and Stout, George L. *Painting Materials: A Short Encyclopedia*. 1942. Reprint. New York: Dover, 1966.

Harley, R. D. *Artists' Pigments c. 1600–1835*. London: Butterworth, 1970.

Hayward, Charles. *Practical Veneering*. London: Evans Bros., 1965.

Huth, Hans. *Lacquer of the West*. Chicago: Univ. of Chicago Press, 1971.

Lamb, F. Bruce. *Mahogany of Tropical America*. Ann Arbor: Univ. of Michigan Press, 1966.

Laurie, A. P. *The Painter's Methods and Materials*. 1960. Reprint. New York: Dover, 1967.

Martin, J. H., and Morgans, W. M. *Guide to Pigments and to Varnish and Lacquer Constituents*. London: Leonard Hill, 1954.

Mayer, Ralph. *The Artist's Handbook of Materials and Techniques*. New York: Viking, 1940.

————. *A Dictionary of Art Terms and Techniques*. New York: Thomas Crowell, 1969.

Merrifield, Mary P. *Original Treatises on the Arts of Painting*. 1849. Reprint. New York: Dover, 1967.

Mills, John, and White, Raymond. "Natural Resins of Art and Archaeology—Their Sources, Chemistry, and Identification." *Studies in Conservation* 22 (1977), 12–31.

Oxford English Dictionary. Compact Edition. London: Oxford Univ. Press, 1971.

The Painter, Gilder, and Varnisher's Companion. Phila.: H. C. Baird, 1850.

Parry, E. J. *Gums and Resins.* London: Pitman, 1918.

————. *Shellac.* London: Pitman, 1935.

Pegler, Martin. *The Dictionary of Interior Design.* New York: Bonanza Books, 1966.

Penn, T. Z. "Decorative and Protective Finishes, 1750–1850." Master's thesis, Univ. of Delaware, 1966.

Remington, J. S. *Drying Oils, Thinners and Varnishes.* London: Leonard Hill, 1946.

Sargent, Charles Sprague. *Manual of the Trees of North America.* 2nd ed. 1922. Reprinted in 2 vols. New York: Dover, 1961.

Shellac. M. Russel, ed. Calcutta: Angelo Bros., 1965.

Sheraton, Thomas. *The Cabinet Dictionary.* 1803. Reprint. New York: Praeger, 1970.

Tingry, P. F. *The Painter's and Colourman's Complete Guide.* London: Sherwood, Gilbert, and Piper, 1830.

————. *The Painter's and Colourman's Complete Guide.* Phila.: E. L. Carey, 1831.

Van de Graaf, J. A. "The Interpretation of Old Painting Recipes." *Burlington Magazine* 104 (1962): 471–75.

Watin, J. F. *L'Art du peintre, doreur, vernisseur.* Paris: Durand, 1776.

THE

Cabinet=Maker's Guide:

OR

RULES AND INSTRUCTIONS

IN THE ART OF

VARNISHING, DYING. STAINING, JAPANNING,
POLISHING, LACKERING AND
BEAUTIFYING

WOOD, IVORY, TORTOISE-SHELL AND METAL.

WITH

OBSERVATIONS ON THEIR MANAGEMENT AND
AP LICATION.

A new edition, with considerable additions.

INCLUDING

AN APPENDIX,

CONTAINING SEVERAL VALUABLE TABLES.

From the latest London Edition.

CONCORD:
PRINTED BY JACOB B. MOORE.
1827.

INTRODUCTION.

—— ✦ ——

NOTHING is more calculated to improve the mechanical arts, than giving publicity to the various processes used among workmen in their several trades; many have been the publications in which various receipts have been given; but in practice not a few have been found to fail, not perhaps because of themselves they were inapplicable, but owing to a want of some practical illustration to enable the workmen to ascertain not only the proportion of the several ingredients, but the method of properly mixing them; and also the proper mode of application, another inconvenience. which, in many instances is a complete bar to the dissemination of practical knowledge is the expensive nature of many works in which valuable receipts are interspersed. The CABINET-MAKER'S GUIDE is, perhaps, the only work that may be properly called a Manual of the Art, and the rapid sale which it met with, is a proof of the estimation in which it was held though even there, much room was left for improvement, particularly in the practical application of the rules and cautions necessary to be observed to ensure success; and many subjects connected with the general plan, still remain untouched: the object of the present work is to embody all that is useful in the Cabinet-Maker's Guide, and adapt to practice what is there given; as well as to enlarge on the original plan, so as to make it a compendium of general practical utility. The various trades of the Cabinet Maker, Chair-Maker, Japanner, Gilder and Lackerer, are so intimately connected. that there is scarce a handsome piece of furniture where the com-

bination of their joint effort is not necessary : and this
inconvenience, if it may be so designated, is particularly felt in country manufactories ; and it is almost
universally the case that a workman in one branch is
entirely ignorant of the methods used by another ; for
instance, the cabinet-maker is, perhaps, generally
speaking, unacquainted with the method to be used in
giving his work the finishing stroke by varnishing or
gilding the several parts, which are necessary to add
to the beauty of the whole : now a knowledge of how
these different operations are performed, even in case
it is put into other hands to finish, will enable him to
leave his part in such a state that the utmost perfection will be attained by those into whose hands it is
to pass for completion ; the present work is therefore
undertaken with a view of supplying what was thought
deficient in the Cabinet-Maker's Guide, and applying
practical illustrations to those receipts where it was
necessary, either to the thorough understanding of the
receipt itself, or showing on what its good or bad
qualities depend

I shall conclude this introduction by pointing out
the characteristics of a good workman and give some
practical rules as concerns the ascertaining the good
or bad qualities of the tools necessary for the trades
to which this publication is more particularly addres-
sed ; and first, it is necessary, in order to form a good
mechanic, that he should strive, with unceasing assi-
duity, to excel in that branch to which his labors are
more particularly directed ; that he should study truth
and accuracy in the several parts, and beauty in the
finishing strokes, in order to atttain these several requisites, he should observe with care the several
methods used by other workmen, and if he can note
down the various operations that contribute to the
excellence of his art, by no means to neglect it, as he
will in time gain a fund of knowledge necessary in his
labors ; with regard to the truth and accuracy of his
work, he should pay particular attention to keep his

tools in proper order, for the time expended in being careful in that respect will be amply repaid by the ease and accuracy with which the several parts of his work will correspond. If careful in this respect, he will save a deal of trouble in the finishing operation, which must be conducted with great care and attention, not attempting to hurry its completion ; as that, in many cases, would act in diametrical opposition to his wishes ; but narrowly to observe the progress he makes, and if any accident should occur, it will mostly be soon remedied ; on the contrary, if with hurry and inattention to any thing but getting the work out of his hands, it will, in many cases, cost him more labor and trouble to repair, than the whole operation would do when conducted with care ; these maxims will not only conduce to make a good mechanic, but what is of as great consequence, a ready workman.

With respect to using the tools used in the trades to which I have alluded, the most necessary, and in which all may be comprehended, are planes, saws and chisels, and we will consider them with respect to the wood they are manufactured from, and the steel which forms the cutting part of them ; and first, beech is in general, and ought to be always used, for the purpose of the stocks, handles, &c.. as it is of a tough texture, and not liable to split or warp so much as any other ; now there are two kinds of beech, usually known by the names of black or red beech, and the white beech, the former is by far the best in every respect, and may be always known by its color, and texture, which is darker and more hard in substance ; the white is more apt to warp, and soon wears with use ; it should therefore always be rejected as improper : again, if you examine a piece of beech end-ways, you will perceive the grain runs in streaks, which, among workmen, is called the beat of the wood ; and in all planes this grain or beat, which is the hard fibrous particles of the wood, should run in a direction perpendicular to the face of the plane, which in that case appears full of

little hard specks ; whereas, if the beat runs parallel
to the face, it will appear in irregular streaks, which
situation of the grain should always be avoided, as
the face will be apt to wear uneven, and more subject
to warp and twist : again in saw-handles, and stocks
for bits, the beat should run in the same direction as
the saw-blade, or in the same as the stock, when laid
on its side ; in moulding planes, it is very frequently
the case, that pieces of box are let into that part of
the face that forms the quirk of the mouldings, but
that, when possible, should be avoided, as the texture
of the two woods are very different, and the different
temperature of the atmosphere will cause a difference
in their contraction, and consequently the plane will
be liable to cast : if it is at any time introduced, I
would recommend only a small piece just at the mouth
of the plane, firmly dove-tailed in, which will not be
so apt to derange the accuracy of the plane.

With respect to saws, chisels, and other edge-tools,
their goodness depends upon the quality of the steel,
which should be uniform throughout, and it is always
better to have them tempered rather too hard than soft,
for use will reduce the temperature ; or if at any time
it is necessary to perform the operation yourself, the
best method I can recommend, is, to melt a sufficient
quantity of lead to immerse the cutting part of the
tool ; having previously brightened its surface, plunge
it into the melted lead for a few minutes, till it gets
sufficiently hot to melt a candle, with which rub its
surface, then plunge it in again, and keep it there till
the steel assumes a straw color ; (but be careful not to
let it turn blue ;) when that is the case, take it out,
rub it again with the tallow, and let it cool ; if it should
be too soft, wipe the grease off, and repeat the process without the tallow, and when it is sufficiently hot,
plunge it into cold spring water, or water and vinegar
mixed : by a proper attention to these directions, and
a little practice, every workman will have it in his
power to give a proper temper to the tools he may use ;

if a saw is too hard, it may be tempered by the same means, but as it would be not only expensive, but. in many cases, impossible to do it at home. a plumber's shop is mostly at hand, where you may repeat the process when they are melting a pot of lead ; but here observe that the temper necessary is different to other cutting tools; you must wait till the steel just begins to turn blue, which is a temper that will give it more elasticity, and at the same time sufficient hard· ness.

With respect to choosing your brushes for varnishing, it is necessary that they possess elasticity combined with softness. and that the hairs are sufficiently fixed, so that taking hold of one hair, it will not pull out or separate from the rest ; the larger brushes are usually made of bristles the smaller of camel's hair ; the former must be firmly tied to the handle, and the string well glued ; the latter are best put into a tin case, and after being used, must always be cleaned according to the directions given in the course of this work.

By paying proper attention to these directions, and a little care, the workman will be enabled to keep his tools in order, and to select such as are proper for the purpose they are intended.

THE

CABINET-MAKER'S GUIDE.

———✦———

Cabinet Work.

———

GENERAL OBSERVATIONS.

AS the beauty of cabinet work depends on the care with which it is finished, I shall, as a proper introductory
article, point out some methods of proceeding which will add much to its beauty, and furnish hints to the workman
for perfecting his art. The usual method of cleaning off any piece of cabinet-
furniture, is simply by scraping and
glass-paper ; which in many instances,
particularly if the grain is any ways
soft, will not produce that face which is
requisite for it to bear a good polish,
either with wax or oil ; another reason
is, that it is difficult at all times to meet
with good glass-paper, which is always
requisite.

To make Glass-paper.

Take any quantity of broken window-glass, that which has rather a green appearance on the edge is best, pound it in an iron mortar, then have two or three sieves of different degrees of fineness, ready for use when wanted ; take any good tough paper, fine cartridge is best, and having levelled the nobs and bumps from both sides with pumice-stone, tack it at each corner on a board, and with good clear glue, diluted with about one third more water than is used generally for wood work, go quickly over the paper taking care to spread it even with your brush ; then, having your sieve ready, sift the pounded glass over it lightly, but to cover it in every part ; let it remain till the glue is set, take it from the board and shake off the superfluous glass again into the sieve, and hang it in the shade to dry : in two or three days it will be fit for use.

Note.—This paper will be much better than any you can buy, as sand is frequently mixed with the glass, and colored to deceive the purchaser.

To make Strong Glue, fit for Inlaying or Veneering.

Take the best glue, which is known by its transparency, and of rather a light brown, and being free from clouds and streaks, dissolve it in the usual quantity of water, and to every quart add one ounce of isinglass and a gill of the best vinegar.

To clean the face of soft Mahogany, or other porous Woods.

After scraping and sand-papering in the usual manner, take a sponge and well wet the surface to raise the grain, and with a piece of fine pumice-stone, free from stony particles, and cut the way of the fibres, rub the wood in the direction of the grain keeping it moist with water ; let the work dry, then if you wet it again you will find the grain much smoother, and it will not raise so much ; if you now repeat the process,

you will find the surface perfectly
smooth, and the texture of the wood, to
appearance, much hardened : by this
means, common soft Honduras mahogany, will have a face equal to the finest
Hispaniola.

Note. —If this does not succeed quite
to your satisfaction, you may still improve the surface, by using the pumice-
stone with cold drawn linseed oil, in the
same manner as you have proceeded
above with water, and this will be found
to put a most beautiful, as well as a durable face to your work, which may
then be polished or varnished as required.

A Glue for Inlaying Brass or Silver Strings, Patteras, &c.

To every pint of common glue take
about the quantity of two table-spoon-
fuls of finely powdered rosin, and the
like quantity of finely powdered brick-
dust, and incorporate the whole well
together ; it will hold the metal much
faster than plain glue, which is generally used.

To take out Bruises in Furniture.

Wet the place well with warm water, then take some brown paper five or six times doubled, and well soaked in water, lay it on the place, apply on that a hot flat-iron till the moisture is evaporated, and if the bruise is not gone, repeat the same ; you will find after two or three applications, the dent or bruise is raised level with the surface ; or if the bruise is small, soak it well with warm water, and apply a red hot poker very near the surface, keeping it continually wetted, and you will soon find the indentation vanished.

Dying Wood.

GENERAL OBSERVATIONS.

It being necessary to say something as to the quality, nature, and texture of the wood most fit for dying, I shall state my remarks in the following order:

First, the wood mostly used to dye black, is pear-tree, holly, and beech, all of which will take a beautiful black; it should at the same time be observed, not to take wood which has been long cut or aged, but as fresh as possible; I have likewise found, that after the veneers have had one hour's boiling, and taken out to cool, that the color has struck much stronger. It should likewise be noticed, that after the veneers are dyed, they should be dried in the air, and not by the fire, or in a kiln of any kind; as it tends to destroy the color.

Secondly, in order to dye blue, green, red, or any other colors, take clear holly; put the veneers first in a box or trough with clean water, and let them remain four or five days, changing the water once or twice, as you may find occasion; the water acting as a purgative in the wood, will bring forth abundance of slime, &c.; let them dry about twelve hours before they are put into the dye; by observing this you will find the color strike quicker, and be of a brighter hue.

Fine Black.

Have a chair-maker's copper fixed, into which put six pounds of chip logwood, and as many veneers as it will conveniently hold, without pressing too tight; fill it with water, and let it boil slowly for about three hours; then add half a pound of powdered verdigris, half a pound of copperas, and four ounces of bruised nut galls, filling the copper up with vinegar as the water evaporates; let it boil gently two hours each day, till you find the wood to be dyed through; which, according to the kind, will be in more or less time.

Fine Blue.

Take a clean glass bottle, into which put one pound of oil of vitriol; then take four ounces of the best indigo, pounded in a mortar into small lumps; put them into the phial (take care to set the bottle in a basin or earthen glazed pan, as it

will ferment ;) after it is quite dissolved,
provide an earthern or wooden vessel,
so constructed that it will conveniently
hold the veneers you mean to dye: fill
it rather more than one third with water,
into which pour as much of the vitriol
and indigo, (stirring it about,) as will
make a fine blue; which you may know
by trying it with a piece of white paper
or wood; put in your veneers, and let
them remain till the dye has struck
through.

Note.—The color will be much better if the solution of indigo in vitriol is
kept a few weeks before using it; also
the best trough you can use, being made
either of common stone, like a stone sink,
but of proper dimensions, say about four
feet by eight or nine inches, which will
be sufficiently large for veneers intended to be stained; or you may procure
one made of artificial stone of any dimension, which will not cost so much;
also you will find the color strike better,
if, previous to putting your veneers into
the blue dye, you boil them in plain water till completely soaked through, and

let them remain a few hours to dry partially previous to immersing them in the dye.

Fine Yellow.

Take of the root of barberry, four pounds, reduce it, by sawing, to dust which put in a copper or brass trough, add four ounces of tumerick, to which put four gallons of water, then put in as many white holly veneers as the liquor will cover, boil them together for three hours, often turning them ; when cool, add two ounces of aquafortis, and you will find the dye strike through much sooner.

Another Yellow much brighter.

To every gallon of water neccessary to cover your veneers, add one pound of French berries, in which boil your veneers till the color has penetrated through ; have ready the following liquid, which add to the infusion of French berries, and let your veneers remain for two or three hours, and you will find the color very bright.

Liquid for brightening and setting the Colors.

Take strong aqua-fortis, a sufficient quantity, and to every pint and one ounce of grain tin, and a piece of sal-al-moniac, of the size of the walnut, setting it by to dissolve, shaking the bottle round, with the cork out, from time to time; in the course of two or three days it will be fit for use.

N. B.—This will be found an admirable liquid to add to any color, as it not only brightens it, but makes it less likely to fade from exposure to the air.

Bright Green.

Proceed as in either of the above receipts to produce a yellow ; but instead of adding aqua-fortis, or the brightening liquid, add the vitriolated indigo, as much as will produce the desired color.

Bright Red.

Take two pounds of genuine Brazil dust, add four gallons of water, put in as many veneers as the liquid will cover,

boil them for three hours; then add two
ounces of alum, and two ounces of aqua-
fortis, and keep it luke warm until it has
struck through.

Another Red.

To every pound of logwood chips add
two gallons of water, put in your veneers, and boil as in the last; then add
a sufficient quantity of the brightening
acid till you see the color to your mind,
keep the whole as warm as you can
bear your finger in it, till the color has
sufficiently penetrated.

Note.—The logwood chips should be
picked from any extraneous substances
with which it generally abounds, as
bark, dirt, &c., and it is always best
when fresh cut, which may be known by
its appearing of a bright red color; for
if it is stale, it will look brown, and will
not yield so much coloring matter.

Purple.

Take two pounds of chip logwood and
half a pound of Brazil dust, add four

gallons of water, and after putting in your veneers, boil them well, for at least three hours ; then add six ounces of pearlash and two ounces of alum, let them boil two or three hours every day, till you find the color struck through.

Note.—The Brazil dust in this receipt is perhaps superfluous, as it only contributes to make the purple of a more red cast, for the pearlash does not act upon it to change it from a red to a purple.

Another Purple.

Take two pounds of logwood, either in chips or powder, and boil it in four gallons of water, along with your veneers ; then after boiling till the color is well struck in, add by degrees some vitriolated indigo till the purple is of the shade required, which may be known by trying it with a piece of paper ; let it then boil for one hour, and keep the liquid in a milk warm state till you find the color has penetrated the veneer. This receipt, when properly managed, will produce a very brilliant purple, which will not be so likely to fade as the foregoing.

Orange.

Let the veneers be dyed, by either of the methods given, of a fine deep yellow, and while they are still wet and saturated with the dye, transfer them to the bright red dye, till you find the color has penetrated equally throughout.

Silver Grey.

Take a cast iron pot of six or eight gallons, and from time to time collect old iron nails, hoops, &c. &c., expose them to the weather till they are covered with rust; add one gallon of vinegar and two of water, boil all well for an hour; then have your veneers ready, which must be air wood, (not too dry,) put them in the copper you use to dye black, and pour the iron liquor over them; add one pound of chip logwood, and two ounces of bruised nutgalls; then boil up another pot of the iron liquor to supply the copper with, keeping the veneers covered, and boiling two hours a day.

Another Grey.

Expose any quantity of old iron, or what is better, the borings of gun barrels, &c. in any convenient vessel, and from time to time sprinkle them with diluted spirits of salts till they are very thickly corroded; then to every six pounds add a gallon of water, in which has been dissolved two ounces of salt of tartar; lay your veneers in the copper, and cover them with this liquid; let it boil for two or three hours till well soaked, then add to every gallon of liquor a quarter of a pound of green copperas, keep the whole at a moderate temperature till the dye has sufficiently penetrated.

—»»o●●««—

Staining.

——

GENERAL OBSERVATIONS.

STAINING differs from the process of dying, inasmuch as it penetrates just below the surface of the wood, instead of colouring its substance throughout, as it does in dying; and the one is used for beautifying the face aiter the work is finished, while the other is employed on the wood before it is manufactured, in the state of veneers, to be cut into strings or bands to be used for inlaying borders, patteras, &c., and which has of late years got much out of use, principally owing to the fault so much complained of, of the colours flying or fading, and which was in consequence of not taking that care in the operation which it required, and in not using any thing but simply the infusion of different colouring materials, wi hout adding any thing to set the colour in the way we have recommended.

Staining is chiefly in use among chairmakers, and when properly conducted and varnished, has a most beautiful appearance, and is less likely to meet with injury than japanning.

Black stain for immediate use.

Boil half a pound of chip logwood in two quarts of water, then add one ounce of pearl-ash, and apply it hot to the work with a brush; take half a pound of logwood and boil it as before in two quarts of water, adding half an once of verdigris, and half an ounce of copperas; strain it off, and put in about half a pound of rusty steel filings and apply as before.

To stain Beech a Mahogany Color.

Take two ounces of dragon's blood, break it in pieces. and put it into a quart of rectified spirits of wine; let the bottle stand in a warm place, shake it frequently, and when dissolved it is fit for use.

Another method for Black Stain.

Take one pound of logwood, boil it in four quarts of water, add a double handful of walnut peeling, boil it up again, take out the chips, add a pint of the best vinegar, and it will be fit for use; apply it boiling hot.

Note.—This will be much improved, if, after it is dry, we take a solution of green copperas dissolved in water, in the proportion of an ounce to a quart, and apply it hot to the above.

To imitate Rose-wood.

Take half a pound of logwood, boil it with three pints of water till it is of a very dark red, to which add about half an ounce of salt of tartar, and when boiling hot stain your wood with two or three coats, taking care that it is nearly dry between each ; then with a stiff flat brush, such as is used by the painters for graining, form streaks with the black stain above named, which if carefully executed, will be very near the appearance of dark rose-wood.

Another Method.

Stain your wood all over with the black stain, and when dry, with a brush as above, dipped in the brightening liquid, form red veins in imitation of the grain of rose-wood. which will produce, when well managed, a beautiful effect.

Note.—A handy brush for the purpose, will be made by taking a flat brush such as is used for varnisning, and cutting the sharp points off the hairs, and making the edge irregular, by cutting out a few hairs here and there, you will have a tool which, without any trouble, will imitate the grain with great accuracy.

To imitate King or Botany-Bay Wood.

Take French berries half a pound, and boil them in two quarts of water, till you have a deep yellow, and with it boiling hot, give two or three coats to your work; let it be nearly dry, then, with the black stain form the grain with your brush: to be used hot.

N. B. You may, for variety, after giving it two or three coats of yellow, give one of strong logwood liquor which will heighten the color, and then use the black stain as directed.

A common Red for Bedsteads and common Chairs.

Archil, as sold at the shops, will produce a very good stain of itself when used cold; but if, after one or two coats being applied and suffered to get almost dry, we brush it over with a hot solution of pearlash in water, it will improve the color.

To stain Horn in imitation of Tortoise-Shell.

Take an equal quantity of quick-lime and red-lead, mix it up with strong soap lees, lay it on the horn with a small brush, in imitation of the mottle of tortoise shell; when it is dry, repeat it two or three times.

Another Method.

Grind one ounce of litharge with half an ounce of quick-lime, to the consistence of paint with a sufficient quantity of liquid salt of tartar, put it on the horn with a brush in imitation of tortoise shell, and in three or four hours it will have produced the desired effect; it may then be washed off with warm water: if not deep enough it may be repeated.

Another Method still better.

Take a piece of lunar caustic, about the size of a pea, and grind it with water on a stone, and mixing with it a sufficient portion of gum arabic to make it of a proper consistence, you may apply it with a brush to your horn, in imitation of the veins of turtle or tortoise shell.

Note.—It would perhaps be as well to mix with it a portion of red lead, or any other powder to give it a body.—This, if properly applied, will stain the horn quite through without hurting its texture or quality; only be careful when the horn is sufficiently stained, to let it be soaked for some hours in plain water previous to finishing and polishing it.

To Stain Musical Instruments.

Fine Crimson.

Take one pound of good Brazil, and boil it in three quarts of water for an hour; strain it, and add half an ounce of cochineal; boil it again for half an hour gently, and it will be fit for use.

If you would have a more scarlet tint, put half an ounce of saffron in a quart of water, boil it for an hour, and pass over the work previous to the red stain.

Purple.

Take a pound of good chip logwood, to which put three quarts of water, boil it well for an hour; then add four ounces of pearlash, and two ounces of indigo pounded, and you will have a good purple.

Fine Black.

In general, when black is required in musical instruments, it is produced by jappanning, the work being well prepared with size and lamp-black; take some black japan, (which is sold at the varnish-makers',) after which varnish and polish it.

Note.—A black stain is sometimes required, as for finger boards, bridges,

&c.; and flutes are sometimes stained, you may then proceed as directed in staining, but the wood ought to be either pear, apple, or box-wood; but the latter is preferable, which may be rubbed over when dry, with a rag or flannel dipped in hot oil, which will give it a gloss equal to ebony.

Fine Blue.

Take a pound of oil of vitriol in a clean glass phial, into which put four ounces of indigo, and proceed as before directed in dying.

Fine Green.

Take three pints of the strongest vinegar, to which put four ounces of the best verdigris pounded or ground fine, half an ounce of sap green, and half an ounce of indigo.

Note.—Perhaps distilled vinegar, or verjuice, would be an improvement.

Bright Yellow.

There is no need whatever to stain the wood, as a very small bit of aloes put into the varnish will make it of a good color and have the desired effect.

To stain Box-wood Brown.

Hold your work to the fire that it may receive a gentle warmth, then take aquafortis, and with a feather or brush, pass over the work till you find it change to a fine brown, (always keeping it near the fire ;) you may then oil and polish it.

Note.—The wood most proper for musical instruments, such as violins, guitars, &c. is air-wood ; or good sycamore, without blemish, when varnished, will look rich.

Varnishing.

GENERAL OBSERVATIONS.

It is the custom, in order to heighten the beauty of fine wood, and give additional lustre to furniture, &c. to to varnish it. The simplicity of the process requires but little to be said on the subject, but that nothing may be wanted to benefit the workman. I shall endeavour, as clearly as possible, to lay down some rules and cautions necessary to be observed, both in making and method of using varnish, that the work may appear as beautiful as possible.

In London it is hardly worth while to make varnish, unless in large quantities, as there are several shops where it may be had very good, and at a fair price; but in the country, where the carraige is an object, and you cannot depend upon the genuineness of the article. it is necessary to be known by the practical mechanic. The varnish in general sold for varnishing furniture, is white and hard varnish.

Cautions respecting the making of Varnish.

As heat in many cases is necessary to dissolve the gums used in making varnish, the best way when practical, is to use what the chemist call a sand bath, which is simply placing the vessel in which the varnish is, in another filled with sand and placed on the fire ; this will generally be sufficient to prevent the spirits catching fire ; but in case of such accidents (which not unfrequently happen.) it will be best to take a vessel sufficiently large that there shall be little danger of spilling any ; indeed, the vessel should never be more than two-thirds filled, but in case of accident, have ready at hand a piece of board sufficiently large to cover the top of the vessel in case of its taking fire, as also a wet wrapper, in case it should be spilt when on fire, as water by itself thrown on it, would only increase the mischief; and the person who attends the varnish pot, should have his hands covered with gloves, and if they are mad of leather, and rather damp, t wie effectually prevent injury. I would particularly impress these cautions on the workman, as from practical knowledge, I have several times witnessed shocking personal injury, from the neglect of these cautions.

*General directions in choosing the Gums
and Spirits used.*

When you purchase a quantity of
gum, first, examine it, and see that it
consists for the most part of clear transparent lumps without a mixture of dirt;
next, when you get it home, select the
clearest and lightest pieces for the most
particular kinds of varnish, reserving
the others, when separated from extraneous matter, for the coarser varnishes.
In choosing spirits of wine, the most
simple test is by immersing the finger in
it, and if it burns quickly out without
burning the finger, it is good ; but if on
the contrary, it is long burning, and
leaves any dampness remaining on the
finger, it is mixed with inferior spirit ;
it may also be compared with other
spirit, by comparing the weight of equal
quantities, the lightest is the best ; the
goodness of spirits of turpentine may
be likewise ascertained in the same manner by weighing it, and by noticing the
degree of inflammability it possesses,
the most inflammable is the best ; and

a person much in the habit of using it, will tell by the smell its good or bad qualities; for the good turpentine has a pungent smell, and the bad a very disagreeable one, and not so powerful.

To varnish a piece of Furniture.

First, observe the work to be clean; then see if any knots or blemishes require filling up, which must be done with cement of the same color; have your varnish in an earthern pot, with a piece of wire diametrically across the top, slackened downwards, to stroke the brush against; then see that your brush is clean, and free from loose hairs, dip your brush in the varnish, stroking it across the wire, and give the work a thin and regular coat; soon after that another, and another, always taking care not to pass the brush twice in the same place; let it stand to dry in a moderately warm place, that the varnish may not chill.

When you have given your work about six or seven coats, let it get quite hard, (which you will prove by pressing your knuckles on it, if it leaves a mark it is not hard enough;) then with the three first fingers of your hand, rub the varnish till it chafes, and proceed over that part of the work you mean to polish, in order to take out all the streaks, or partial lumps made by the brush; give it then another coat, and let i stand a day or two to harden.

Note. —The best vessel for holding your varnish is commonly sold at color-shops, called a varnish pan; it is constructed of tin with a false bottom; the intervail between the two bottoms is filled with sand, which being heated over the fire, keeps the varnish fluid and flows more readily from the brush; there is a tin handle to it, and the false bottom comes sloping from one end to the other, which causes the varnish to run to one end, and with a wire across in the same manner as recommended in the above directions.

To keep your Brushes in order.

The brushes used for varnishing are

either flat in tin, or round tied firm to the handle, and either made of camel's hair or very fine bristles; in the use of which it is necessary to be very careful in cleaning them after being used, for if laid by with the varnish in them they are soon spoiled; therefore after using them wash them well in spirits of wine or turpentine, according to the nature of your varnish; after which you may wash them out with hot water and soap, and they will be as good as new, and last a great while with care; and the spirits that are used for cleaning, may be used to mix with varnish for the more common purposes, or the brushes may be cleaned merely with boiling water and strong yellow soap.

To make the best white hard Varnish.

Rectified spirits of wine, two gallons; gum sandrach, five pounds; gum mastic, one pound; gum anime, four ounces; put these in a clean can, or bottle to dissolve, in a warm place, frequently shaking it, if (when the gum is dissolved) you strain it trough a lawn sieve, it is fit for use.

To make Mastic Varnish proper for varnishing Pictures or Drawings.

To every quart of spirits of turpentine put one pound and a quarter of the cleanest gum mastic, set it in a sand-bath till it is all dissolved, then strain it through a fine sieve, and it is ready for use; if too thick, you may thin it with spirits of turpentine.

To make Turpentine Varnish.

To one gallon of spirits of turpentine add five pounds of clear rosin pounded; put it in a tin can, on a stove, and let it boil for half an hour; when the rosin is all dissolved, let it cool, and it is fit for use.

To make a varnish for Violins, &c.

Take half a gallon of rectified spirits of wine, to which put six ounces of gum mastic, and half a pint of turpen-

tine varnish ; put the above in a tin
can, keep it in a very warm place, frequently shaking it, until it is dissolved ;
strain it and keep it for use. Should
you find it harder than you wish, you
may add a little more turpentine varnish.

*To varnish Harps and Dulcimers in the
Indian manner.*

Prepare the work with size and red
ochre ; then take ochre, burnt umber,
and red-lead, well ground, and mix up
a dark brown color in turpentine varnish, adding so much spirits of turpentine that you may just be able to work
it, pass over your work fair and even ;
and while it is yet wet, take a muslin
sieve, and sift as much Dutch metal,
(bronze,) upon it, as you think requisite to produce the effect ; after which
varnish and polish it.

*To varnish Drawings. or any kind of Pa-
per or Card-work.*

Take some clear parchment cuttings,

boil them in water in a clean glazed pipkin, till they produce a very clear size, strain it, and keep it for use.

Give your work two coats of the above size, passing quickly over the work, not to disturb the colors, proceed as before directed with your varnish.

Another Method still better.

Take one ounce of the best isinglass, dissolve it in about a pint of water by simmering it over the fire ; strain it through fine muslin, and keep it for use.

Try the size on a piece of paper, (heat it to a moderate heat,) and if it glistens it is too thick ; then add more water, if it soaks into the paper it is too thin ; add or diminish the isinglass till it merely dulls the surface ; then take your drawing, and give it two or three coats, being careful (particularly in the first coat) to bear very lightly on the brush, (which should be a flat tin camel's hair,) and plenty of size to flow freely from it, otherwise you may damage the drawing.

Then take the best mastic varnish and give it at least three coats, and the effect will answer your most sanguine wishes.

Note.—This is the method used by many eminent artists, and is found superior to any that has been tried.

Amber Varnish.

Take amber eight ounces, in powder, and two of gum lac : melt the amber by means of heat, in a glazed pipkin, with half a pint of the best spirits of turpentine ; and when melted, add the gum lac, place it on the fire again, and keep stirring it with a piece of wood till it is all dissolved, then add one ounce of the clearest cold-drawn linseed oil ; stir it well together, and strain it for use.

Oil Varnish.

Take any quantity of the best linseed oil, let it boil for an hour, then to every pound of oil add a quarter of a pound of the clearest rosin in powder. stir it well till dissolved; then add for every pound of oil used, one ounce of spirits of turpentine, strain it and bottle for use.

Note.—This is a cheap and good varnish for sash frames. or any work where economy is required; it has besides the property of bearing hot water without being damaged, and is not subject to crack or scratch.

Copal Varnish.

Take spirits of wine one quart, gum copal one ounce, and shell lac half an ounce; reduce the gums to powder, put the spirits in a jar or bottle, add the gums, place the whole in a warm place, with the cork lightly in the bottle; shake it occasionally, and when the gums are quite dissolved, strain and bottle for use.

Japanning.

GENERAL OBSERVATIONS.

It frequently happens that japanned work receives damage, when it is very inconvenient (either from distance or other circumstances) to send for a japanner to repair it, therefore it may not be improper to lay down the most simple methods used in that branch.

First, provide yourself with a small muller and stone, to grind any color you may require.

Secondly, provide yourself with white hard varnish, brown varnish, turpentine varnish, japan gold size, and spirits of turpentine, which you may keep in bottles for the purpose.

Thirdly, provide yourself with flake white, red-lead, vermillion, lake, Prussian blue, king's and patent yellow, orpiment, spruce and brown ochre, mineral green, verditer, burnt umber, and lamp-black, to which may be added raw sienna, and burnt sienna, with the best yellow ochre and light red (or burnt ochre) and Vandyke brown.

Observe—That all your wood work must be prepared with size, and some coarse material mixed with it to fill up and harden the grain of the wood, (such as may best suit the color intended to be laid on,) which must be rubbed smooth with glass-paper when dry ; but in case of *accident,* it is seldom necessary to resize the damaged places, unless they are considerable.

With the foregoing colors you may match almost any color now in use in japanning, always observing to grind your colors smooth in spirits of turpentine ; then add a small quantity of turpentine and spirit-varnish, lay it carefully on with a camel's-hair brush, and varnish it with brown or white spirit varnish, according to the color.

Note. -You will find a box filled with currier's shavings useful for cleaning your stones and pallet with, for they should never be laid by dirty. as a great deal depends on the beauty of the work in keeping all your colors separated, and that before you grind another color, the first should be well wiped off your stone.

For a black Japan.

Mix a little gold size and lamp-black, it will bear a good gloss without varnishing over.

To imitate black Rose-wood.

To work must be grounded black, after which take some red lead, well ground. and mixed up as before directed, which lay on with a stiff flat brush, in imitation of the streaks in the wood ; after which take a small quantity of lake, ground fine, and mix it with brown spirit varnish, carefully observing not to have more color in it than will just tinge the varnish ; but should it happen, on trial, to be still too red, you may easily assist it with a little umber ground very fine ; with which pass over the whole of the work intended to imitate black

Rose-wood, and it will have the desired effect.

It well done, when it is varnished and polished it will scarcely be known from Rose-wood.

Note.—Instead of the Umber in the above, you may use a small quantity of Yan*yke brown, as it is much more transparent than the Umber.

—➤●●◀—

Polishing.

GENERAL OBSERVATIONS.

FIRST, the varnish for cabinet-work should be very clear and bright, otherwise it will give a dingy shade to all light-colored woods.

Secondly, some persons polish with rotten stone, others with putty powder, and I have seen varnish polished with common whiting and water ; but Tripoli will be found to answer the best.

To polish Varnish.

It has been considered by many as a matter of difficulty, they have furnished themselves with a quantity of materials, and as often fa'led of success, the process being rather tedious.

Take two ounces of Tripoli powdered, put it in an earthern pot or basin, with water to cover it ; then take a piece of fine flannel four times doubled, lay it over a piece of cork or rubber, and proceed to polish your varnish, always wetting it with the Tripoli and water ; you will know when the process is done, by wiping a part of the work with a sponge, and observe whether there is a fair and even gloss ; take a bit of mutton suet and fine flour and clean off the work.

Caution.—You must be careful not to rub the work too hard, nor longer than is necessary to make the face perfectly smooth and even.

The French method of Polishing.

Take a piece of fine pumice-stone

and water, and pass regularly over the work with the grain, until the rising of the grain is down ; then take powdered Tripoli and boiled linseed oil. and polish the work to a bri.ht face, which will be far superior to any other polish, but it requires much more time.

To polish brass ornaments inlaid in Wood.

First, carefully observe to have your brass work filed very clean with a smooth file ; then take some tripoli, powdered very fine, and mix it with linseed oil, and with a rubber made from a piece of old hat, or felt, you may polish the work as you would polish varnish, until you have the desired effect.

If the work is ebony or black rose wood, take some elder-coal, powdered very fine, and apply it dry after you have done with the Tripoli; it will produce a superior polish.

To polish Ivory.

Ivory is best polished with putty and water, by means of a rubber made of hat, which in a short time produces a fine gloss.

To polish any work of Pearl.

Take pumice-stone, finely powdered, (and washed to separate the impurities and dirt,) with which you may polish it very smooth ; then take putty powder as directed for ivory, and you will have a fine gloss and a good color.

Friction varnishing, or French polishing.

GENERAL OBSERVATIONS.

THE method of varnishing furniture, by means of *rubbing* it on the surface of the wood, is of comparatively modern date, though bees'-wax has been used either by itself, or mixed with spirits of turpentine for a very considerable period, for that purpose, and which at first produces a very good gloss, though it does not wear well, and is particularly liable to spot with wet, and look smeary when touched with the fingers; to remedy these inconveniencies, and put a harder face, which shall not be so liable to scratch as varnish, and yet have an equally fine face, the French polish was introduced, and as it would be unpardonable in a work like this, to omit a full direction of the process, and also the various preparations of the different compositions necessary, it is here introduced that nothing might be wanting to make this work as complete as possible.

All the polishes are used pretty much in the same way, therefore a general description will be a sufficient guide for the workman. If your work is porous, or the grain coarse, it will be necessary, previous to polishing, to give it a coat of clear size previous to your commencing with the polish, and when dry, gently go over it with very fine glass-paper, the size will fill up the pores and prevent the waste of the polish, by being absorbed into the wood; and also a saving of considerable time in the operation. Place your work so that the light may shine on it in an ob ique direction to enable you to see by looking sideways, how the polishing proceeds.

Make a wad with a piece of coarse flannel or drugget, by rolling it round and round, over which, on the side meant to polish with, put a very fine linen rag several times doubled, to be as soft as possible, put the wad or cushion to the mouth of the bottle containing the preparation, (or polish,) and shake it, which will damp your rag sufficiently. then proceed to rub your work in a circular direction, observing not to do more than about a square foot at a time; rub it lightly till the whole surface is covered, repeat this three or four times, according to the texture of the wood ; each coat to be rubbed until the rag appears dry, and be careful not to put too much on the rag at a time, and you will have a very beautiful and lasting polish ; be also very particular in letting your rags be very clean and soft, as the polish depends in a great measure on the care you take in keeping it clean and free from dust during the operation.

The True French Polish.

To one pint of spirits of wine, add a quarter of an ounce of gum copal, a quarter of an ounce of gum arabic, and one ounce of shell-lac

Let your gums be well bruised, and sifted through a piece of muslin. Put the spirits and the gums together in a vessel that can be close corked, place them near a warm stove, and, frequently shaking them, in two or three days they will be dissolved; strain it through a piece of muslin and keep it tight corked for use.

An improved Polish.

Take a pint of spirits of wine, add, in fine powder, one ounce of seed lac, two drachms of gum guaicum, two drachms of dragon's blood, and two drachms of gum mastic; expose them in a vessel stopped close, to a moderate heat for three hours, until you find the gums dissolved ; strain it off into a bottle for use, with a quarter of a gill of the best linseed oil to be shaken up well with it.

Note.—This polish is more particularly intended for dark-colored woods, for it is apt to give a tinge to light ones, as satin-wood, or air-wood &c. owing to the admixture of the dragon's-blood, which gives it a red tinge.

Water Proof Polish.

Take a pint of spirits of wine, two ounces of gum benzoin, a quarter of an ounce of gum sandrach and a quarter of an ounce of gum anime ; these must be put into a stopped bottle, and placed either in a sand-bath or in hot water till dissolved, then strained ; and, after adding about a quarter of a gill of the best clear poppy oil, and well shook up, put by for use.

Bright Polish.

A pint of spirits of wine to two ounces of gum benzoin and half an ounce of gum sandrach, put in a glass bottle corked, and placed in a sand-bath. or hot water, until you find all the gum dissolved, will make a beautiful clear polish for Tunbridge ware goods, tea-caddys, &c ; it must be shaken from time to time, and when all dissolved, strained through a fine muslin sieve and bottled for use.

Prepared Spirits.

This preparation is useful for finishing after any of the foregoing receipts, as it adds to the lustre and durability as well as removing every defect which may happen in the other polishes; and it gives the surface a most brilliant appearance.

Half a pint of the very best rectified spirits of wine, two drachms of shellac, and two drachms of gum benzoin. Put these ingredients in a bottle, and keep it in a warm place till the gum is all dissolved, shaking it frequently; when cold, add two tea-spoonfuls of the best clear white poppy oil, shake them well together and it is fit for use.

This preparation is used in the same manner as the foregoing polishes, but, in order to remove all dull places, you may increase the pressure in rubbing.

Strong Polish.

To be used in the carved parts of cabinet-work with a brush, as in standards, pillars, claws, &c.

Dissolve two ounces of seed-lac, and two ounces of white rosin in one pint of spirits of wine.

This varnish or polish must be laid on warm, and if the work can be warmed, also, it will be so much the better; at any rate, moisture and dampness must be avoided.

Directions for cleaning and polishing Old Furniture.

Take a quart of stale beer or vinegar, put a handful of common salt, and a table-spoonful of spirits of salt, boil it for a quarter of an hour; you may keep it in a bottle, and warm it when wanted for use; having previously washed your furniture with soft hot water to get the dirt off, then polish, according to the directions, with any of the foregoing polishes.

Cleansing.

To clean and restore the elasticity of cane Chair-bottoms, Couches, &c.

TURN up the chair-bottom, &c. and with hot water and a sponge, wash the cane work well, so that it may be well soaked, should it be dirty you must add soap; let it dry in the air, and you will find it as tight and firm as when new, provided the cane is not broken.

To clean old brass-work, for Lackering.

First boil a strong lye of wood ashes, which you may strengthen by soap lees;

put in your brass-work, and the lacker will immediately come off; then have ready a pickle of aqua fortis and water strong enough to take off the dirt, wash it immediately in clean water, dry it well and lacker it.

To clean Silver Furniture.

Lay the furniture, piece by piece, upon a charcoal fire, and when they are just red take them off and boil them in tartar and water, and your silver will have the same beauty as when first made.

A receipt to clean Marble, Sienna, Jasper, Porphyry, Sciola, &c.

Mix up a quantity of the strongest soap-lees with quick lime, to the consistency of milk, and lay it on the stone, &c. for twenty-four hours, clean it afterwards with soap and water, and it will appear as new.

Note.—This may be improved by rubbing or polishing it afterwards with fine putty powder and olive oil.

To take Ink spots out of Mahogany.

Apply spirits of salt with a rag, until the spot disappears, immediately wash with clear water.

Another Method.

To half a pint of soft water, put an ounce of oxalic acid, and half an ounce of butter of antimony; shake it well, and when dissolved will be very useful for extracting stains out of mahogany, as well as ink, if not of too long standing.

------❖●●●❖------

Silvering.

GENERAL OBSERVATIONS.

THE art of silvering looking-glasses, or plate glass, when conducted in the large way, requires great care and practice, and is almost a trade of itself, and the apparatus necessary very expensive, therefore not worth the while of

any one's undertaking without a considerable business in that way; but for the
sake of the mechanic, I will endeavor
to explain the process which may be
conducted in the small way, particularly when at a distance from London, with
advantage by the cabinet-maker, who
by-the-by ought to combine the several
trades of that with carver and gilder, as
well as japanner and varnisher, for it is
seldom in a country town that they are
thought of as separate trades, therefore
every thing in the furniture way is sent
to the cabinet-maker to be made or re-
paired; the requisites necessary are,
first, a large stone or plate of cast iron
made perfectly smooth and level. Secondly, a sufficient number of square
lead or iron weights of from seven to
fourteen pounds weight each. Thirdly,
a quantity of tin foil. And, lastly,
good distilled quicksilver, free from any
impurities, for on the goodness of it, depends the beauty of the silvering.

Method of Silvering Looking-Glasses and Plate Glass.

Having your stone or plate firmly fixed on a strong table, spread your tin foil smoothly and evenly on it to the size of the plate you intend to silver, then take your quicksilver and pour it on the foil, spread it evenly and smoothly with a hare's foot, that it may adhere to the foil in every part, lay a smooth piece of strong blotting paper on it, and on that your plate to be silvered, shoving it on from one end, that the air may not be included between that and the glass; now draw the paper gently and regularly from between the plate and glass, and place your weights side by side, as the paper is withdrawn, till the glass is entirely covered; elevate the stone at one end, which will cause the superfluous silver to run from between the glass and foil, let it remain in that position for about a week or ten days, and taking off your weights, you will find (if the process has been conducted with care) it silvered to your mind.

Note.—The stone should have a groove round the top. that the superfluous silver can run to the bottom, from whence it may be taken to use for the same purpose again.

To make liquid foil for silvering glass Globes, Bent Mirrors, &c.

Take one ounce of clean lead, and one ounce of fine tin, melt them together in a clean iron ladle, then immediately add one ounce of bismuth, skim off the dross, remove the ladle from the fire, and before it sets add ten ounces of quicksilver; stir the whole carefully together observing not to breathe over it, as the evaporation of the quicksilver is very pernicious.

Another Method.

Take four ounces of quicksilver, to which put as much tin foil as to become barely fluid when mixed ; have your globe, or bent mirror, clean and warm, and either inject the quicksilver by means of a clean earthern pipe at the

aperture, turning it about till it is silvered all over, or, if a bent mirror, pour it
gently into it, turn it about till the silver
adheres all over, let the remainder run
out, and hang it up.

Bronze and Painting.

To Bronze Figures.

For the ground, after it has been siz-
ed and rubbed down, take Prussian blue,
verditer and spruce ochre, grind them
separately in water, turpentine, or oil,
according to the work; mix them together in such proportions as will produce the color you desire; then grind
Dutch metal, commonly called bronze,
in the same material you ground your
color: laying it with judgment on the
prominent parts of the figure it will produce a grand effect.

Note. —There are several different
colors of Bronze which are best imita-
ted by the powders, independent of the

one here mentioned of Dutch metal,
and are made not without considerable
trouble, by dissolving different metals in
aquafortis, and precipitating the solution by means of sal-ammoniac, and
washing the precipitate in water, and
drying it on blotting-paper; the ingenious artist will suit the color of the
bronze, by mixing corresponding colors
of paint for a ground.

Green Paint for Garden Stands, Vene-tian Blinds, Trellisses, &c.

Take mineral green and white lead
ground in turpentine, mix up a quantity
to your mind, with a small quantity of
turpentine varnish for the first coat ; for
the second, you must put as much varnish in the color as will produce a good
gloss.

Note.—By adding a small quantity of
Prussian blue, you will have the color
much brighter.

Gilding.

GENERAL OBSERVATIONS.

GILDING on wood is performed in two
different ways, and is called oil gilding
when the process is performed by means
of oil or varnish, and is well calculated
for out-door work, as it will stand the
weather and bear washing: the other,
and by far the most beautiful, is that
employed for picture frames, furniture,
&c. and is called burnish gilding, which,
when well executed, adds greatly to the
ornamental work often introduced, either
in the internal decoration of rooms, or
the carved work and reeding in furniture. As both these methods are so
necessary to the workman, I shall be
particular in laying down such rules and
directions, that with a little care and
practice the ingenious mechanic will
soon be able to execute any piece of
work wherein the assistance of gilding
is necessary, and where a regular gilder is not at hand.

Necessary Requisites to be provided with.

First, a sufficient quantity of leaf gold, which is of two sorts, the high gold as it is called, and the pale gold; the former is much the best, but the latter very useful as being of a different color, you may introduce, if necessary, a variety; it is also cheaper, therefore to be preferred where expense is an object.

Secondly, A gilder's cushion, which is an oblong piece of wood, covered with a piece of what the book-binders call rough calf-skin, and is stuffed with flannel several times doubled; and a border of parchment, about four inches deep at one end, to prevent the air blowing the leaves about when taken from the book and placed on the cushion.

Thirdly, A gilding knife, with a straight and very smooth edge, to cut your gold in the pieces necessary.

Fourthly, Several camel-hair pencils, of different sizes, and some tips. as they are called, which is a few long camel's hairs put between two cards in the same manner that the hairs are put into tin

cases for brushes, making, as it were, a
flat brush, with a very few hairs.

Lastly, A burnisher, which is a crook-
ed piece of agate set in a long wooden
handle.

To make Size for preparing your Frames, &c.

Take half a pound of parchment
shavings, or cuttings of white leather;
add three quarts of water, and boil it
in a proper vessel till it is reduced to
nearly half the quantity; take it off the
fire and strain it through a sieve: be
careful in the boiling to keep it well stir-
red, and do not let it burn.

To prepare your Frames or Wood-work.

First, with the above size alone, and
boiling hot go over your frames in every
part; then take a sufficient quantity of
whiting and mix with some size, to the
consistence of thick cream; go over every part of your frame, and give it six
or seven coats, carefully letting each
coat dry before you proceed with the

next, and you will have a white ground
fit for gilding on nearly, or quite, the
sixteenth of an inch in thickness.

Note.—You must not have your size
too thick, and it need not be put on,
when mixed with the whiting, so hot as
the first coat is by itself; it will be better in order to separate the dirt or coarse
parts of the whiting, to strain it through
a sieve. Vauxhall whiting is the best.

Polishing.

When the prepared frames are quite
dry, proceed to clean and polish them;
wet a small piece at a time, and take a
smooth fine piece of cloth dipped in water, rub the part till all the lumps and
inequalities are removed, and for those
parts where the fingers will not enter the
mouldings, &c. wind the wet cloth round
a piece of wood adapted to the moulding or quirk, by this means you will
make the surface all smooth and even
alike.

Note.—Where there is carved work,
&c. it will sometimes be necessary to

bring the mouldings to their original sharpness, by means of chisels, gouges, &c. as the preparation will be apt to fill up all the finer parts of the work which must be thus restored; it has sometimes been the practice, after polishing to go over the work once with fine yellow or Roman ochre, but in general this is hardly necessary.

Gold Size.

Take fine boll-ammoniac, what quantity you please, grind it fine with a muller and stone, scrape into it a little beef suet, grind all well together; after which mix in with a pallet-knife, a small proportion of parchment size with a double proportion of water.

Another Gold Size.

Take a lump of tobacco-pipe clay, and grind it into a very stiff paste with thin size; add a small quantity of ruddle, and fine black lead ground very fine, and temper the whole with a small piece of tallow.

To prepare your Frames &c for Gilding.

Take a small cup, or pipkin, in which put as much gold size as you judge sufficient for the work in hand, add parchment size, till it is just sufficient to flow from the brush; when quite hot. pass over your work with a very soft brush, taking care not to put the first coat too thick; let it dry, and repeat it twice or three times more, and when quite dry, brush the whole with a stiff brush, to remove any nobs, &c. that there may have been in the size : your work is now ready for applying the gold.

Note.—Your parchment size should be of such consistence, when cold, as the common jelly sold in the shops ; for if too thick it will be apt to chip, and if too thin will not have sufficient body.

Laying on the Gold.

This is the most difficult part of the operation, and requires some practice ; but I shall endeavor so to describe the method that, with a little caution and attention it may be easily performed.

Turn your gold out of the book on your cushion a leaf at a time ; then passing your gilding knife under it, bring it into a convenient part of your cushion for cutting it into the size of the pieces required ; breathe gently on the centre of the leaf, and it will lay flat on your cushion ; then cut it to your mind by bringing the knife perpendicularly over it and sawing it gently, it will be divided.

Place your work before you, nearly horizontal, and with a long-haired camel-hair pencil, dipped in water, (some use a small quantity of brandy in the water,) go over as much of your work as you intend the piece of gold to cover ; then take up your gold from your cushion by means of your tip ; by drawing it over your forehead or cheek, it will damp it sufficiently to adhere to the gold which must then be carefully transfered to your work, and gently breathing on it, it will be found to adhere ; but you must mind that the part you apply it to is sufficiently wet ; indeed it must be floating, or you will find the gold apt to crack; proceed in this manner by a little at a time and do not attempt to cover too much at a time, till you find by experience you are able to handle your gold with freedom. Be careful in proceeding with your work, if you find any flaws or cracks appear, to take a corresponding piece of gold, and apply it immediately; sometimes also, you will find it necessary when your gold does not appear to adhere sufficiently tight to draw a pencil quite filled with water close to the edge of the gold, that the water may run underneath it, which will answer your expectation.

Burnishing.

When your work is covered with gold set it by to dry, it will be ready to burnish in about eight or ten hours; but it will depend on the warmth of the room or state of the air, and practice will enable you to judge when to seize the proper time.

When it is ready, those parts which you intend to burnish must be dusted with a soft brush, and wipe your burnisher with a piece of soft wash leather, quite dry; begin to burnish about an inch or two in length at a time, taking care not to lean too hard, but with a gentle and quick motion, apply the tool till you find it all over equally bright.

Matting.

Those parts of your work which look dull from not being burnished, are now to be matted, that is, are to be made to look like dead gold; for if left in its natural state it will have a shining appearance which must be thus rectified:

Grind some vermillion, or yellow ochre, very fine, and mix a very small portion, either with parchment size, or with the white of an egg, and with a very soft brush lay it even and smooth on the parts intended to look dull; if well done, it will add greatly to the beauty of the work.

Note.—The work must be well cleared of superfluous gold, by means of a soft brush, previous to burnishing or matting.

Finishing.

All that is now necessary is to touch the parts in the hollows with a composition called vermille; it is made by grinding vermillion, gamboge, and red lead, very fine, with oil of turpentine, and applying it carefully with a small brush in the parts required, and your work is completed.

Note.—Sometimes the finishing is done by means of shell-gold, which is far the best method, it should be diluted with gum arabic, and applied with a small brush.

To make Shell-gold.

Take a quantity of gold leaf, and grind it with a small portion of honey, to a fine powder; take a little gum arabic and sugar candy, with a little water, and mix it well together, put it in a shell to dry against you want it.

Silver Size.

Take tobacco pipe clay, grind it fine with a little black lead and Genoa soap, and add parchment size as directed for gold size.

Note.—Any soap would most probably answer as well as Genoa soap; but I have made it as here directed, and found it answer very well.

Silvering.

Silvering is at present but little in use, though I have seen some old works that still looked very well, and I think might be introduced with advantage in many works; the great fault is, that it is apt to tarnish, but which may be preserved with very little dimunition to its beauty, by applying a thin coat of the cleanest copal or mastic varnish. The process for silvering is exactly the same as for gold, but the matting must be done by mixing a small quantity of flake white, in powder, with a little prussian blue (just sufficient to tinge it) along with plain size or white of egg.

Lackering.

THE art of lackering is so nearly allied to that of japanning that it is scarcely necessary to say much as to its application; however, as some directions may be thought necessary, I will endeavour to explain shortly the process.

If the work is old, clean it according to the directions given under the article *Cleaning*; if new, it will require nothing but being freed from dust, and well rubbed with a piece of wash leather to make it bright as possible. Have a hot plate, or for want of which, the hob of your fire place will be a good substitute; lay your brass work on it till moderately heated, but not too hot, for that will blister your lacker; then, according to the color you wish, take any of the following preparations, and making it warm, lay hold of your brass work with a pair of pincers or pliers, and with a soft brush apply the lacker, being careful not to rub it on, but stroke the brush

gently one way, and place your work on
the hot plate again till the varnish is
hard; but do not let it remain too long,
experience will best tell you when it
should be removed; (some indeed never place it on the stove or plate a second time;) if it should not be quite covered, you may repeat it carefully, and
if pains be taken with your lacker, it will
look equal to metal gilt.

To make Gold Lacker for Brass.

Take of rectified spirits of wine, two
quarts; and three pounds of seed lac,
picked particularly clean and clear of
all black and brown specks and pieces,
as upon that depends entirely the beauty of the lacker; add them together,
keep them warm, and shake them often:
when the lac is dissolved, it is fit for
use.

Another Method.

Take of the clearest and best seed
lac one pound, of dragon's blood one
ounce, pound them well together; add

a pint and a half of the best spirits of wine, set it in a warm place to dissolve, strain it, and it is fit for use.

A pale Gold Lacker.

Dissolve in a pint of spirits of wine, as much gamboge as will give it a bright yellow, then add three quarters of a pound of seed-lac, finely powdered and sifted, set it in a sand-bath to dissolve : when that is the case, bottle and stop it well till wanted for use.

Buhl Work.

GENERAL OBSERVATIONS.

It is a term of modern date, applied to the art of *Inlaying* with turtle or tortoise-shell, with brass or silver, and when well executed, has a most beautiful effect. I shall endeavor to furnish the workman with such practical directions, that I trust will soon enable the ingenious mechanic to accomplish that which has hitherto been chiefly monopolized by foreigners, but which, in my opinion, only wants some familiar directions, and practical instructions, to enable our artists to equal, if not outdo their rivals.

The chief difficulty seems to be in the proper mode of cutting out the pieces for inlaying, and the method of veneering the work when the several pieces are cut out.

To prepare your Shell and Brass ready for cutting out.

Being furnished with a thin plate of brass, of the usual thickness of a veneer, or as thin as can be conveniently worked, make the faces on both sides rough with a coarse file, or tooth plane, and also a veneer of shell of the dimensions requisite, tooth that also; then warm your plates and veneers, pass a coat of glue first over a plate of brass; place over that a thin sheet of paper, glue that and place your shell veneer on the top; place them between two smooth and even boards, either kept down by a heavy weight, or squeezed tight together with hand screws; let them remain till dry, when they will be found to adhere together sufficiently tight.

Cutting out your veneer.

Having drawn the pattern you intend on your shell; or, if it will not appear sufficiently plain, paste a piece of paper on its surface, and let it dry, on which draw your design; being now provided with a bow-saw, the blade of which is very thin and narrow, such as may be made with a watch-spring, cut into about six strips, and the stretcher of the frame at a sufficient distance from the blade to enable you to turn in any direction, according to your pattern, and all made extremely light, begin by making a small hole in your veneer in a part where it will not be so much observed, (unless the pattern comes quite out to the edge,) and invert your saw; then very carefully follow the lines of your pattern till it is all cut through; you

will then have two pieces, which may
be again separated by exposing them to
steam or warm water; then take the
two corresponding pieces, one of brass
and one of shell, and when glued together according to the following direction, you will have two veneers, the
counterparts in pattern with each other,
only where the brass is in one, the shell
will be in the other.

To glue up your Pattern.

Take two boards of sufficient dimensions and heat them before the fire, and
rub them well with tallow to prevent
the glue sticking to it; take a sheet of
paper, on which lay your veneer, and
having well rubbed some strong glue
into the vacancies where the pattern is
to be inserted, put it carefully in its
place, rubbing it down with a veneering hammer, over which place another
sheet of paper; place the whole between the hot boards, and press or screw
them together with hand-screws; let
them get quite dry, they will come out

quite clean from the boards, and appear as one piece of veneer; you may then scrape the paper clean off, it is then ready for laying or applying to your work.

Laying your Veneer.

Having made your work perfectly level with a tooth-plane, apply to your veneer the glue recommended under the article *Cabinet Work*, and lay it on your work; then with a hot board, termed a call, fasten it well down by means of hand-screws, and let it remain till perfectly hard. It then only remains to be cleaned off and polished, according to the directions given under the article *Polishing*.

Note.—In order to add to the beauty of your work, and produce a variety in the shade, it is necessary, before laying your veneer, to give that side intended to be glued, a coat or two of some color ground in oil, or varnish, and set by to dry thoroughly before you lay your veneer, as red-lead and vermillion ground together; king's yellow, Prussian blue, or any color you may fancy; and sometimes the sheet is gilt on the side which you intend to lay on your work, this produces a most brilliant effect, and even the common Dutch metal applied will have a good effect.

The method here given for tortoise-shell and brass, is equally applicable to woods of two different colors, only then you need not use any other glue but that in common use, which must be good.

───◦◦●◦●◦◦───

Cements.

To make Cement Mahogany color.

TAKE two ounces of bees'-wax. half an ounce of rosin, melt them together; then add half an ounce of Indian red, a small quantity of yellow ochre, to bring it to the color you desire : keep it in a pipkin for use.

Portable Glue, or Bank-note Cement.

Take one pound of the best glue, boil and strain it very clear; boil likewise four ounces of isinglass, put it into a double glue pot, with half a pound of fine brown sugar, and boil it pretty thick; then pour it into plates or moulds: when cold, you may cut and dry them for the pocket.

Note.—This glue is very useful to draftsmen, architects, &c. as it immediately dilutes in warm water, and fastens the paper without the process of damping; or it may be used by softening it in the mouth, and applying it to the paper.

Cement for Turners.

Take bees'-wax one ounce, rosin half an ounce, and pitch half an ounce, melt them together, and stir in it some very fine brick-dust to give it a body; if too soft add more rosin, if too hard, more wax: when nearly cold, make it up into cakes or rolls, which keep for use.

Note.—This will be found very useful for fastening any piece of wood on your chuck, which is done by applying your roller of cement to the chuck while going round ; it will melt the cement, then apply the piece of wood you wish to affix to the chuck, and it will adhere with sufficient force.

To make Cement for broken Glass.

Take one ounce of isinglass, steep it in half a pint of spirits of wine, for twenty-four hours, then let it dissolve over a slow fire, always keeping it covered, or the spirit will evaporate ; then take six cloves of garlic, bruise them well in a mortar, put them in a linen cloth, and squeeze the juice into the isinglass, mix all well together and keep it for use, it being excellent to join glass ornaments, &c. &c.

Miscellaneous.

To make black Wax.

TAKE two ounces of bees'-wax, half an ounce of Burgundy pitch, melt them together, then add one ounce and a half of ivory black ground very fine and dried.

Green Wax.

Take two ounces of bees'-wax, melt it, add one ounce of verditer; let the pipkin be large enough as it will immediately boil up; stir it well, and add one quarter of an ounce of rosin: it will be sufficiently hard and fit for use.

To make furniture paste.

Scrape four ounces of bees'-wax into a pot or basin; then add as much spirits of turpentine as will moisten it through; at the same time powder a quarter of an ounce of rosin and add to it; when it is dissolved to the consistence of paste, add as much indian red as will

bring it to a deep mahogany color: stir
it up and it is fit for use.

Another Method.

Scrape four ounces of bees'-wax as
before, then take a pint of spirits of
turpentine in a clean glazed pipkin, to
which add an ounce of alkanet root, cover it close and put it over a slow fire,
attending it carefully that it may not boil,
or catch fire ; and when you perceive
the color to be drawn from the root, by
the liquid being of a deep red, add
as much of it to the wax as will moisten
it through; at the same time add a quarter of an ounce of powdered rosin, cover it close, let it stand six hours, and it
will be fit for use.

To make Furniture Oil.

Take linseed oil, put it in a glazed
pipkin, with as much alkanet root as it
will cover; let it boil gently, and you
will find it become of a strong red color:
let it cool, and it will be fit for use.

Another Method.

Boil together cold drawn linseed oil and as much alkanet root as it will cover and to every quart of oil, add two ounces of the best rose pink; when all the color is extracted, strain it off, and for every quart add a gill of spirits of turpentine: it will be a very superior composition for soft and light mahogany.

To soften Ivory.

Slice a pound of mandrake, and put it in a quart of the best vinegar, into which put your ivory; let it stand in a warm place for forty eight hours; you will then be able to bend the ivory to your mind.

To bleach Ivory.

Take a double handful of lime, and slack it by sprinkling it with water, then add three pints of water, and stir it up together; let it settle ten minutes, and pour the water into a pan for your purpose; then take your ivory, and steep it in the lime water twenty four hours, after which boil it in strong alum water one hour, and let it dry in the air.

To solder or weld Tortoise-Shell or Horn.

Provide yourself with a pair of pincers or tongs, so constructed that you can reach four inches beyond the rivet; then have your tortoise-shell filed clean to a lap joint, carefully observing that there is no grease about it; wet the joint with water, and you will find the shell to be joined as it were one piece.

To gild Leather for Bordering Doors, Folding Screens, &c.

Take a quantity of clear brown sheepskins, damp them with a sponge and water, and strain them tight, with tacks, on a board sufficiently large; when dry, size them with clear double size; then take the white of eggs, beat them with a whisk to a foam, and let them stand to settle; then take books of leaf silver, a sufficient quantity, and blow out the leaves of silver on a gilder's cushion; pass

over the leather carefully with the egg
size, and with a tip brush lay on your
silver, closing any blister with a bit of
cotton; when dry varnish them over
with yellow lacker till they are of a
fine gold color; your skins being thus
gilt, you may then cut them in strips
as you please, and join them with paste
to any length.

Observe—To perform the foregoing
operation in the height of summer, when
the air is clear, dry and warm, that the
skins may dry well before you size them,
and the size may have the desired effect
upon the pores, and no farther. and that
the silver may not tarnish before you
lacker it.

To Damask Leather for Table Covers, &c.

Provide yourself with a block, glued
up, two feet six inches long, and two
feet wide, faced with pear tree, (or box
is still better,) five eights of an inch
thick, upon which have some handsome
pattern drawn, that has a good effect in
light and dark shades only ; but it must

be divided, so that it will match end for end, and side for side; which pattern must be then cut in relief in the same manner as the blocks for printers or paper-stainers, and may be done by any one who knows a little of chair-carving; then strain your leather, dry, on the blocks with tacks, (face upwards,) and with a glass ball rubber of about four pounds weight, pass to and fro over the leather, rubbing hard till you produce the pattern perfectly glazed on the leather.

Note.—If your cover is larger than the block, you must be very careful in shifting it, that you may not injure the pattern.

If from your wood block you have a pattern cast in brass, and nicely touched up by an engraver, and fixed on a block of wood, it will answer much better, and the pattern will come off much sharper and cleaner.

To make Parchment Transparent.

Take a thin skin of parchment and soak it in a strong lye of wood ashes, often wringing it out till you find it become transparent, then strain it on a frame and let it dry.

Note.—This will be much improved, if after it is dry, you give it a coat. on both sides, of clear mastic varnish diluted with spirits of turpentine.

To make Composition Ornaments for Picture Frames, &c.

Take any quantity of whiting, as much as you think you shall have occasion for. for the present use, mix it up with thinnish glue to the consistence of putty, and having a mould ready, rub it well all over with sweet oil, and press your composition in it; take it out and you will have a good impression, which you must set by to dry, or if wanted, you may, before it gets hard, apply it to your work with thick glue. and bend it into the form required for the angles of your frames, &c.

Note.—If you have not a mould at hand, you may make one of the composition from any leaf or pattern you may wish to copy, and letting it get quite hard, use it as a mould, first oiling it well.

You will find this composition of great use for copying any pattern you may wish from good models.

To imitate Wood, &c. for internal or external Decorations.

Having prepared your wood of a proper ground with a common oil paint, prepare the color for the graining, by grinding, very fine, with stale beer, the color you require, using this in the manner of distemper, or drawing in water colors; let it get quite dry, and give it two of these coats of clear copal varnish.

An excellent receipt for Burnish Gold Size.

One ounce of black lead, ground very fine, one ounce of deer suet, one ounce of red chalk, and one pound of pipe-clay, ground with weak parchment size to a stiff consistence, to be used as directed under the article *Gilding.*

Note.—This receipt is by an excellent practical workman.

To clean Pictures.

Having taken the picture out of its frame, take a clean towel and making it quite wet, lay it on the face of your picture, sprinkling it from time to time with clear soft water, let it remain wet for two or three days, take the cloth off and renew it with a fresh one ; after wiping your picture with a clean wet sponge, repeat the process till you find all the dirt soaked out of your picture ; then wash it well with a soft sponge, and let it get quite dry ; rub it with some clear nut or linseed oil, and it will look as well as when fresh done.

Another Method.

Put into two quarts of strong lye, a quarter of a pound of Genoa soap, rasped very fine, with about a pint of spirits of wine ; let them simmer on the

fire for half an hour, then strain them
through a cloth, apply it with a brush
to the pictures, wipe it off with a sponge,
and apply it a second time, which will
effectually remove all dirt ; then with a
little nut oil, warmed, rub the picture
and let it dry ; this will make it look as
bright as when it came out of the artist's
hands.

To silver Clock Faces, Scales of Barometers, &c.

Take half an ounce of old silver
lace, add an ounce of the best aqua-fortis, put them in an earthern pot, and
place them over a gentle fire till all is
dissolved, which will happen in about
five minutes, then take them off and mix
it in a pint of clear water, after which,
pour it into another vessel, and free it
from sediment ; then add a spoonful of
common salt, and the silver will be precipitated in the form of a white powder
or curd, pour off the acid and mix the
curd with two ounces of salt of tartar,
half an ounce of whiting and a large

spoonful of salt ; mix it up together, and it is ready for use.

In order to apply the above composition, clean your brass or copper plate with some rotten stone and a piece of old hat; rub it with salt and water with your hand, take a little of the composition on your finger and rub it over your plate, and it will firmly adhere and completely silver it, wash it well with water ; when dry, rub it with a clean rag and varnish it.

Note.—This silver is not durable, but may be improved by heating the article and repeating the operation till the covering seems thick enough.

Varnish for Clock Faces, &c.

Take of spirits of wine one pint, divide it into four parts, mix one part with half an ounce of gum mastic, in a bottle by itself ; one part of spirits, and half an ounce of gum sandrac in another bottle ; and one part of spirits and half an ounce of the whitest part of gum Benjamin, mix and temper them to your mind ; if too thin, some mastic ; if too soft, some sandrach or Benjamin when you use it, warm the silvered plate before the fire, and with a flat camel-hair pencil, stroke it over till no white streaks appear, and this will preserve the silvering for many years.

Crystallized Tin.

Take sheet tin, the best and thickest covered with the metal you can get, clean it well with whiting and water till the face is well polished ; warm it or lay on a hot plate, and with a sponge or brush wet it well with strong spirits of salts, you will soon see it shoot into beautiful patterns ; as soon as this happens, plunge it into cold spring water ; you may then varnish it with any color you please, or leave it in its natural state and varnish with clear varnish.

Note.—This has of late been much introduced into furniture, and, when well executed, has a beautiful appearance ; you may use it as a veneer in a manner directed for buhl work, having first given the side you intend to be glüed to your work a good coat of paint.

Size for Oil Gilding.

Grind calcined red ochre, with the best and oldest drying oil, and mix with a little oil of turpentine when used.

Note.—When you intend to gild your work, first give it a coat of parchment size ; then apply the size where requisite, either in patterns or letters, and let it remain till by touching it with your fingers it will just feel sticky ; apply your gold leaf, and dab it with a piece of cotton ; let it remain for about an hour, and wash the superfluous gold off with a sponge and water, and, when dry, varnish it with copal varnish.

General Directions for Dying Ivory or Bone.

First, let them be soaked for about twelve hours in lime water ; take them out and immerse them in weak aqua-fortis for about two or three hours ; you may then proceed as in dying wood, only be careful not to let your dye be too hot.

The method of gilding the borders of the Leather Tops of Library Tables, Work Boxes, &c.

The tops of library tables, &c. are usually covered with Morocco leather, and ornamented with a gilt border, and are usually sent to a book binder for that purpose. The method by which they perform it is as follows:—They first go over that part intended to be gilt with a sponge dipped in the glare of eggs, which is the whites beaten up to a froth and left to settle; and the longer made or the older it is, so much the better; then being provided with a brass roller, on the edge of which the pattern is engraved, and fixed as a wheel in a handle, they place it before the fire till heated so that, by applying a wetted finger, it will just hiss; while it is heating, rub the part with an oiled rag, or clean tallow, where the pattern is intended to be, and lay strips of gold on it, pressing it down with cotton; then with a steady hand, run the roller along the edge of the leather, and wipe the superfluous gold off with an oiled rag, and the gold will adhere in those parts where the impression of the roller has been, and the rest will rub off with the oiled rag.

APPENDIX.

—∞∞—

IN order to render the Cabinet-Makers Guide a complete Pocket Manual for the workman, as well as a book of reference, it has been thought that the addition of some useful Tables would not be unacceptable in a work of this nature.

The following have, therefore, been contrived, and will show, by inspection, the superficial content of any board or plank, without having recourse to duo-decimals or cross multiplication ; and will enable any one at all acquainted with the simple rules of arithmetic, to find the content sufficiently accurate for any practical purpose, though they might have been extended to show the fractional parts of inches to any degree of accuracy required.

Explanation of Tables 1 and 2.

TABLE 1.—If we call the left hand column feet, and the top row inches, all

TABLE I.

Inches in Width.

Feet or Inches in length	2	3	4	5	6	7	8	9	10	11	12
1	0:2	0:3	0:4	0:5	0:6	0:7	0:8	0:9	0:10	0:11	1:0
2	0:4	0:6	0:8	0:10	1:0	1:2	1:4	1:6	1:8	1:10	2:0
3	0:6	0:9	1:0	1:3	1:6	1:9	2:0	2:3	2:6	2:9	3:0
4	0:8	1:0	1:4	1:8	2:0	2:4	2:8	3:0	3:4	3:8	4:0
5	0:10	1:3	1:8	2:1	2:6	2:11	3:4	3:9	4:2	4:7	5:0
6	1:0	1:6	2:0	2:6	3:0	3:6	4:0	4:6	5:0	5:6	6:0
7	1:2	1:9	2:4	2:11	3:6	4:1	4:8	5:3	5:10	6:5	7:0
8	1:4	2:0	2:8	3:4	4:0	4:8	5:4	6:0	6:8	7:4	8:0
9	1:6	2:3	3:0	3:9	4:6	5:3	6:0	6:9	7:6	8:3	9:0
10	1:8	2:6	3:4	4:2	5:0	5:10	6:8	7:6	8:4	9:2	10:0
11	1:10	2:9	3:8	4:7	5:6	6:5	7:4	8:3	9:2	10:1	11:0
12	2:0	3:0	4:0	5:0	6:0	7:0	8:0	9:0	10:0	11:0	12:0

TABLE II.

Parts of Inches in Width.

	1	$\frac{1}{8}$	$\frac{1}{4}$	$\frac{3}{8}$	$\frac{1}{2}$	$\frac{5}{8}$	$\frac{3}{4}$	$\frac{7}{8}$
2		0:$\frac{1}{4}$	0:$\frac{1}{2}$	0:$\frac{3}{4}$	1:0	1:$\frac{1}{4}$	1:$\frac{1}{2}$	1:$\frac{3}{4}$
3		0:$\frac{3}{8}$	0:$\frac{3}{4}$	1:$\frac{1}{8}$	1:$\frac{1}{2}$	1:$\frac{7}{8}$	2:$\frac{1}{4}$	2:$\frac{5}{8}$
4		0:$\frac{1}{2}$	1:0	1:$\frac{1}{2}$	2:0	2:$\frac{1}{2}$	3:0	3:$\frac{1}{2}$
5		0:$\frac{5}{8}$	1:$\frac{1}{4}$	1:$\frac{7}{8}$	2:$\frac{1}{2}$	3:$\frac{1}{8}$	3:$\frac{3}{4}$	4:$\frac{3}{8}$
6		0:$\frac{3}{4}$	1:$\frac{1}{2}$	2:$\frac{1}{4}$	3:0	3:$\frac{3}{4}$	4:$\frac{1}{2}$	5:$\frac{1}{4}$
7		0:$\frac{7}{8}$	1:$\frac{3}{4}$	2:$\frac{5}{8}$	3:$\frac{1}{2}$	4:$\frac{3}{8}$	5:$\frac{1}{4}$	6:$\frac{1}{2}$
8		1:0	2:0	3:0	4:0	5:0	6:0	7:0
9		1:$\frac{1}{8}$	2:$\frac{1}{4}$	3:$\frac{3}{8}$	4:$\frac{1}{2}$	5:$\frac{5}{8}$	6:$\frac{3}{4}$	7:$\frac{7}{8}$
10		1:$\frac{1}{4}$	2:$\frac{1}{2}$	3:$\frac{3}{4}$	5:0	6:$\frac{1}{4}$	7:$\frac{1}{2}$	8:$\frac{3}{4}$
11		1:$\frac{3}{8}$	2:$\frac{3}{4}$	4:$\frac{1}{8}$	5:$\frac{1}{2}$	6:$\frac{7}{8}$	8:$\frac{1}{4}$	9:$\frac{5}{8}$
12		1:$\frac{1}{2}$	3:0	4:$\frac{1}{2}$	6:0	7:$\frac{1}{2}$	9:0	10:$\frac{1}{2}$

(left margin label: Feet or Inches in Length.)

the other columns will show their products in feet and inches: thus supposing
we have a board 8 feet long and 7 inches
broad, the meeting of the horizontal
row at 8, and the perpendicular column
at 7, will be expressed thus—4:8; which
is, that the superficial content of such
board is 4 feet 8 inches ; and so of any
other.

If we call the left hand perpendicular column inches, and we wish to find the content of a piece of wood 9 inches by 7 inches, look at the meeting of the corresponding columns to 9 and 7 for the answer 5:3, which is 5 superficial inches and three parts, or twelfths of an inch.

TABLE II.—Is exactly upon the same principle; thus if we wish to find the content of 11 feet, by $\frac{5}{8}$ of an inch, we shall (by carrying our eye horizontally from 11 to where it meets the perpendicular column marked $\frac{5}{8}$) find 6:$\frac{7}{8}$; that is, 6 inches and $\frac{7}{8}$ of an inch superficial.

I might have given another table for parts of inches by parts of inches; but in real practice this can be but very seldom required, and in general the measurement of a board or plank is not taken nearer than half or quarter inches, and that only in the width, as when the plank is long in comparison to its width, the fraction of an inch would make but very little difference.

The following example will show the use of the tables to those unacquainted with cross multiplication:—

Required the superficial content of a board 11 feet 7 inches, by 5 feet 3½ inches.

	Ft.	In.
1st, 11 ft. multiplied by 5 ft., is	55	0
2d, 11 ft. by 3 inches, by table I.	2	9
3d, 11 ft. by ½ an inch. table II. is	0	5½
4th, 5 ft. by 7 inches, table I. is	2	11
5th, 7 inches by 3 inches, table I. is	0	$1\frac{9}{12}$

which, added together, is equal to 61 $2\frac{1}{2}$ $\frac{9}{12}$

Note.—The same example, worked by cross multiplication, would be equal to not quite ½ a superficial inch more than here given; a quantity of inconsiderable magnitude.

Explanation of Table III.

TABLE III—Is continued for readily computing the content of trees, according to the common method of measuring timber; viz. by taking the girth and dividing it into four equal parts, and is thus

TABLE III.

In.	Ft.	Ins.	Ins.	Ft.	Ins.	Ins.	Ft.	Ins.	Ins.	Ft.	Ins.	Ins.	Ft.	Ins.	Ins.	Ft.	Ins.
6	0	3	9	0	6¾	12	1	0	15	1	6¾	18	2	3	21	3	0¾
¼	0	3¼	¼	0	7	¼	1	0½	¼	1	7¼	¼	2	3¾	¼	3	1½
½	0	3½	½	0	7½	½	1	1	½	1	8	½	2	4½	½	3	2½
¾	0	3¾	¾	0	8	¾	1	1½	¾	1	8¾	¾	2	5¼	¾	3	3½
7	0	4	10	0	8¼	13	1	2	16	1	9¼	19	2	6	22	3	4¼
¼	0	4¼	¼	0	8¾	¼	1	2¼	¼	1	10	¼	2	6¾	¼	3	5¼
½	0	4½	½	0	9	½	1	3	½	1	10¾	½	2	7½	½	3	6
¾	0	5	¾	0	9½	¾	1	3¾	¾	1	11¼	¾	2	8½	¾	3	7
8	0	5¼	11	0	10	14	1	4½	17	2	0	20	2	9¼	23	3	8
¼	0	5½	¼	0	10½	¼	1	5	¼	2	0¾	¼	2	10	¼	3	9
½	0	6	½	0	11	½	1	5½	½	2	1½	½	2	11	½	3	10
¾	0	6¼	¾	0	11½	¾	1	6	¾	2	2¼	¾	2	11¾	¾	3	11

used :—Seek in the first column (or the
other columns marked inches, and en-
closed between double lines) the length
of the quarter girth ; take out the opposite number and multiply that number
by the length of the tree in feet, &c. the
product will be the content in solid feet,
&c.

The following example will show its
utility :—

What is the content in solid feet, &c.
of a tree whose length is 9 feet, and the
quarter girth 16¼ inches.

	Ft.	Ins.
In the table, opposite 16¼, is	1	10
which, multiplied by 9		9
The content is therefore equal to	16	6

Note.—The method here shown will,
in general, be within an inch or two of
the true measure as given by the usual
method, and will not only be found very
ready, but sufficiently accurate, for most
practical purposes.

TABLE IV.

Hundredth parts of a foot.		Inches & 12th parts		Inches & 8th parts		Hundredth parts of a foot.
	1	0	1	0	1	1
	2	0	3	0	2	2
	3	0	4	0	3	3
	4	0	6	0	4	4
	5	0	7	0	5	5
	6	0	9	0	6	6
	7	0	10	0	7	7
	8	1	0	1	0	8
	9	1	1	2	0	17
	10	1	2	3	0	25
	20	2	5	4	0	33
	30	3	7	5	0	42
	40	4	10	6	0	50
	50	6	0	7	0	58
	60	7	2	8	0	67
	70	8	5	9	0	75
	80	9	7	10	0	83
	90	10	10	11	0	92
	100	12	0	12	0	100

Explanation of Table IV.

TABLE IV. will be found very useful for changing feet decimally divided into inches and parts of an inch. and the contrary ; by means of which dimension taken either way may be readily changed to the other; an example in each case will show its utility.

Example 1. To change 56 hundredth parts of a foot into inches and parts.

In the first column, opposite 50, is 6 | 0, and opposite 6. is 0 | 9, which added to the former is six inches and nine twelfths of an inch.

Example 2. To change 10¾ inches into hundredth parts of a foot.

In the column on the right of the double line marked inches and eighth parts, we find opposite 10 inches 83, and opposite ¾ (that is six eighths) is 6, which added to 83, gives 89 hundredth parts of a foot.

TABLE V.

Measures of different Countries.	Parts.	Ft.	In.	Lin	Pts.
English	1440	1	0	0	0
Amsterdam	1335	0	11	1	5
Berlin	1428	0	11	10	8
Brussels	1299	0	10	9	9
China (Imperial Ft.)	1513	1	0	7	3
Constantinople	1678	1	1	11	8
Copenhagen	1511	1	0	7	1
Dantzic	1329	0	11	0	9
Denmark	1508	1	0	6	8
Florence	1433	0	11	11	3
Genoa (the Palm)	1170	0	9	9	0
Hamburgh	1343	0	11	2	3
Leghorn	1428	0	11	10	8
Leipsic	1489	1	0	4	9
Lisbon	1371	0	11	5	1
Madrid	1319	0	10	11	9
Moscow	1337	0	11	1	7
Naples (the Palm)	1240	0	10	4	0
Paris (the Foot)	1535	1	0	9	5
—— (the Metre)	4731	3	3	5	1
Riga	1342	0	11	2	3
Rome (the Palm)	1055	0	8	9	5
Stockholm	1545	1	0	10	5
Venice	1638	1	1	7	8
Vienna	1492	1	0	5	2
Warsaw	1684	1	2	0	4

Explanation of Table. V.

TABLE V. will be found very useful for changing the different measures of foreign countries to that of England, and the contrary ; and is a selection from a very extensive one given by Dr Hutton in his Mathematical Recreations, and needs no explanation ; but that the second column is calculated as the supposition, that the English foot is divided into 12 inches and each inch into 12 parts called lines, and each line into 10 parts, making 1440 parts in the English foot; and the foot of all other countries contains the number of the same parts they are equal to, when compared to the English foot.

French Measures.

The English foot is to the Paris foot, as 1 to 1·065977.

The English square foot is to the Paris, as 1 to 1·136307.

The English cube foot is to the Paris, as 1 to 1·211277.

PRACTICAL RULES, &c. FOR FINDING THE
SUPERFICIAL CONTENT OR AREA OF PLAIN
FIGURES AND SOLID BODIES.

1. *The Diameter of a Circle being given, to
find the Circumference.*

RULE.—As 7 is to 22, or as 113 is to
355, so is the diameter taken in any dimension, as feet, inches, &c. to the circumference in the like measure.

2. *The Diameter of a Circle being given, to
find the Area or Superficial Content.*

RULE.—Find the circumference by
the first rule, then multiply half the circumference by half the diameter, and
the product will be the area.

Note.—For practical purposes you
may measure the circumference with a
string, and half that length multiplied
by half the diameter is the area.

3. *Any Sector of a Circle being given to
find the Area.*

RULE.—Measure the arc with a string;
then half that measure multiplied by the
radius of the circle (of which the arc is
a portion) is the area required.

4. *To find the Area of an Ellipsis or Oval.*

RULE.—Multiply the longest diameter

by the shortest, and the product by the decimal ·7854.

5. *To find the Area of a Triangle.*

Rule, Multiply the length of the base by the perpendicular altitude of the triangle, and half that product is the area.

RULE 2.—When the length of the three sides are only given, from half the sum of the three sides subtract each side severally; multiply the half sum and the three remainders continually together; then extract the square root of the last product, and it will give the area required.

. *To find the area or Superficial Content of a Globe.*

RULE 1.—Multiply the circumference by the diameter and the product is the superfices or area.

RULE 2.—Multiply the diameter of the globe by itself, and the product by 3·14159 for the area.

7. *To find the Area of a Cylinder.*

RULE.—Multiply the length by the circumference; this will give the area of the curved surface, to which add the area of the circle at each end, (by Rule

2,) and you have the whole superficial content of the cylinder.

8. *To find the Superficial Content of a Cone.*

RULE.—Multiply half the circumference at the base, by the slanting height, it will give the curved surface of the cone, to which add the area of the circle at the base, and you will have the whole superficies.

9. *To find the Solidity of a Sphere or Globe.*

RULE.—Find the surface, (by Rule 6) multiply that by the sixth part of the diameter, and you have the solid content.

10. *To find the Solid Content of a Pyramid.*

RULE.—Multiply the area of the base by the perpendicular height, and divide that product by 3 for the solid content.

11. *To find the Solid Content of a Cylinder.*

RULE.—Multiply the area of one end (found by Rule 2) by the length, and the sum is the solid content required.

TABLE VI.

Weight of a Cube Foot of	lb.	oz.	
Oak	57	13	925
Oak heart of, very old	73	2	1170
Cork	15	0	240
Elm Plank	41	15	671
Ash ditto	52	13	845
Beech	53	4	852
Alder	50	0	800
Walnut	41	15	671
Willow	36	9	585
Male Fir	34	6	550
Female Fir	31	2	498
Poplar	23	15	383
Apple Tree	49	9	793
Pear ditto	41	5	661
Quince ditto	44	1	705
Medlar	59	0	944
Plum Tree	49	1	785
Cherry Tree	44	11	715
Filbert Tree	37	8	600
French Box	57	0	912
Dutch ditto	83	0	1328
Dutch Yew	49	4	788
Spanish ditto	50	7	807
Spanish Cypress	40	4	644
American Cedar	35	1	561
Pomegranate Tree	84	10	1354
Spanish Mulberry	56	1	897
Lignum Vitæ	83	5	1333
Orange Tree	44	1	705

EXPLANATION OF TABLE VI.—The only part that requires to be explained in this table is the right hand column, which expresses the comparative weight of the different woods, the weight of a cubic foot of river water being 1.000, and these numbers also express the number of avoirdupois ounces in a cubic foot, supposing the wood to be well seasoned, and free from knots.

INDEX.

Cabinet Work.

Dying Wood.

Staining.

To Stain Musical Instruments.

Varnishing.

Bronze and Painting.

Gilding.

Lackering.

Buhl Work.

Cements.

Miscellaneous.